Subjective Reality: Are You In or Out?

Dara Fogel, Ph.D.

For all those who Seek.

CONTENTS

ACKNOWLEDGMENTS

There are many who have contributed to the manifesting of this work, all deserving of gratitude and obeisance. Many thanks to: Tom Boyd, Ed Sankowski, Tom Burns, Michelle Bresee, Steve Pavlina, Timothy Leary, John Lilly, G.I. Gurdjieff, Seth and Jane Roberts, Robert Scheinfeld, Wayne Dyer, Esther and Abraham- Hicks, Marianne Williamson, Joseph Chilton Pearce and Terence McKenna and many, many others.

I would especially like to thank Richard Auer, Julian Auer and Joane Fogel for putting up with me!

CHAPTER 1
INTRODUCTION

This volume contains ten essays written over the past two decades, exploring different aspects of Subjective Reality and connecting to the Deep Self. Some of the material has been previously published on my website, www.province-of-the-mind.com, but much has never been published or made publically available until now.

Some of the essays were written when I was in graduate school, some written in the years since, but all of them are wrestling with articulating the ineffable.

As a result, some of the essays cover the same ground, but from slightly different perspectives. Some of the essays were meticulously researched, while others were essentially channeled from my own sources. Some of the essays are formal and academic, while others are more casual and personal. The first six essays are written as stand alone pieces, while the last four chapters were written as one work.

I do not pretend to have answers for anyone else, but I have tried to the best of my ability to express and explore my own interior, subjective experience.

A book of this type is a tricky undertaking, as anything I might say to you is merely my own opinion. And if I am the only consciousness that exists, why am I bothering to explain it?

I have a twofold response: firstly, by trying to put my first-hand experience into words that others who have not had similar experiences can understand, I am challenged to analyze and organize my thoughts and understanding in a more linear fashion – an exercise which yields its own rewards in greater comprehension.

And secondly, if I am an aspect of the One Consciousness, as I experience myself to be, then my task is that of an alarm clock. This small aspect of the One is seeking to enlarge its connection with the greater whole by incorporating ever more into my identity.

In other words, if I can get YOU to wake up, then, since you are also a small aspect of that larger Self that I am, we both and the whole world benefits from your increased awareness

It is my hope that you will find some hints, clues, tips and practical information here that will help speed you on your way to greater realization.

Namaste,

~Dara

CHAPTER 2
OBJECTIVE OR SUBJECTIVE: WHAT IS THE TRUE NATURE OF REALITY?

As I see it, there are only two viable possibilities for the nature of reality and how it relates to our personal experience of life. Either reality is completely external to us - something we are born into and have very limited control over (this view is known as **Objective Reality)**; Or it is internal, meaning all of reality is a projection of our inner being, which is known as **Subjective Reality**, (close variants are Monism, Non-dualism or Solipsism). These are the two extreme and polar positions. It is possible to posit a third alternative of some combination of external and internal, but for reasons I will elucidate in a bit, I do not believe that is a viable possibility.

So why is the question of the true nature of reality even important?

Because how we answer this question determines everything, literally EVERYTHING we experience on personal, cultural and global scales.

Conscious Critters

You are a conscious critter - you are aware of yourself as a distinct entity. We humans are all conscious critters, with varying degrees of self-awareness. All of our experience is filtered through our consciousness for interpretation, evaluation and response. Therefore, the only way we are capable of knowing reality is through the mediation of our consciousness - that is, subjectively.

This has led to what is known in philosophy as "the Problem of Other Minds." We experience our own consciousness directly, but we cannot directly experience the consciousness of someone else. We can only infer their consciousness from their behaviors. We can't crack open their skulls and peer inside to see what they are *really* thinking.

Nor can we perform a Vulcan Mind Meld to join consciousness with others. And science is no help here, because it can't even figure out what consciousness is, much less how it relates to reality. So while it might seem reasonable to assume that others are conscious, we really have no way of proving it without using consciousness as the primary means to determine consciousness - a bootstrap maneuver if I ever heard one!

So, if there is no way to prove that other people are conscious, to assume that they are is a huge leap of faith based on some pretty shaky evidence. Yet our culture makes this assumption and even takes it farther. Not only does mainstream society believe that everyone, all 7 billion+ of us, are conscious, it also assumes that all of reality (other consciousness & all) are located outside of us. In other words, we were 'born into' this already on-going reality that has been cranking along for billion of years, and we have very limited influence on this external reality that existed long before us and will continue to exist long after we are gone.

Each of these conscious critters, according to mainstream thought, has it's own subjective way of experiencing the world and interpreting those experiences, but somehow, we manage to agree enough on our interpretations to mostly get along. This is know as **Intersubjective Agreement**. It is where our interpretations of our experiences differ that we clash. Nobody knows where our consciousness comes from or really how or why it functions. But we all seem to have one and they are all different and unique.

So, according to mainstream thought, we all are trapped alone inside our own subjective minds while also being thrown into an external reality that we have very little control over. Sounds pretty sucky to me. Now mainstream thought does not offer any explanations *why* this should be so, nor any proof. All it does is assume and assert this is 'how it is - like it or lump it.'

But what if this assumption is wrong?

Subjective Reality: the Alternate Possibility

Subjective Reality does not necessarily assume there is an external, objective reality. This view holds that consciousness is all there is, and that all consciousness is unitive - that is, there are no pesky other minds to become a problem. There is only one ultimate mind that is the source and originator of all subjective experience - as the Hare Krishnas would say, one 'Ultimate Enjoyer,' and it is YOU.

Not your ego-self you, or your physical body you, but rather the consciousness which is observing and experiencing you. What I like to call the Inner Being or Inner Self. It is this Inner Being which is the Ultimate Consciousness. Most of us are only dimly aware of this inner self, because unless conscious effort is made to contact it, it is content to sit and watch and enjoy the ride. This inner being you is the source and creator, as well as experiencer, of your existence, according to this view.

It can be likened to a dream:

Your everyday world is the Dream, and your 'actual' Self (capital S) is the Dreamer. So the self (small s) you experience inside the Dream is actually only a fraction of the much larger Self who is doing the Dreaming.

Everything you experience is a part of the Dream, and therefore, your own creation and connected to you, from the level of the Dreamer.

Subjective reality only takes as real what it experiences first-hand, since external or objective reality is not seen as a reliable report, coming from second-hand sources. This approach is also known as Gnosticism - the seeking of direct knowledge (Gnosis), rather than accepting external reports as knowledge without personal experience.

It is just as impossible to provide proof of the validity of Subjective Reality as it is to prove objective reality, as any proof I could give would just be a second-hand report, not first-hand experience. BUT... The subjective reality model DOES solve several problems that the objective model of reality can't.

For example, Subjective Reality solves the Problem of Other Minds by saying that there AREN'T any other minds - we just think there are. And this also explains why we do not have direct access to the minds of others (like through mind melds or some technology) - because there's nothing there to access except ourselves.

OK, I hear you say. If I am the only consciousness that exists, how come I don't know all this directly?

Because that would spoil the fun! Where would be the mystery in discovering yourself if you already knew before you started? Also, we are brainwashed at an early age by our culture that punishes us harshly if we dare to posit a different interpretation of reality.

But, I hear you ask, if I am all that exists, that is, if my inner being is the source of all of my experience, then why would I put myself through all the misery and suffering of ignorance and fear? Why would I create an environment hostile to learning about my own true nature? If I am the source of everything, and everything is set up to somehow benefit me, how am I benefitted by experiencing fear, loneliness and weakness?

Why do you go to the movies or theater? Why do you watch or participate in sports? Why read books or watch tv? Most people will say they do those things for entertainment. But why do we want to be entertained? We enjoy being entertained, right? We can still enjoy a well-played game, even if our team loses. We enjoy a good story, even if it's hard on the protagonists of the story. In fact, the more contested the game, the more complicated and heart-wrenching the story, the more we seem to like it.

SUBJECTIVE REALITY: Are You In or Out?

This is a major question for the subjective approach to answer. Many dismiss consideration of the subjective approach because they cannot imagine a satisfactory response to these very valid questions.

And this is where objectivity fails. For any response I give to you will be necessarily a second-hand report, which you would still need to verify by your own personal experience, which would necessarily be different from my own experience. But, I am forced to turn to subjectivity to continue the discussion. My own personal experiences are the only thing that can convince me of the rightness or wrongness of an approach to understanding reality. My personal experiences support and affirm the subjective view much more than they support and affirm the external reality view.

Philosophers (and many others, including scientists) hate and disparage subjective reality for exactly this reason. They feel it leads to selfishness and egoism. But, actually, if you already *are* everything, what need do you have to be selfish, as you already have everything - *you just need to realize and accept it*. Rather, if the true nature of reality is unitive, then the goal becomes to actively realize its oneness, not to further fragment it.

Don't Mess with Mr. In-Between

Why are the only choices Objective or Subjective? Why isn't there some combination of the two - a subjective universe that still has objective aspects? There are some that posit this view, and it is the basis of Cartesian Dualism.

This approach doesn't make sense to me - Either I am everything or I am not everything. Either the UNI-verse is unitive or it is fragmented - there is no in-between. To be unitive is to be subjective and to be objective is to be fragmented into billions of different consciousnesses.

"The One and the Many" - that ancient puzzle of the Pre-Socratic Philosophers has never really been resolved. Is there only one thing in the Uni-verse, or are there many things in the Multi-verse? Is it one song or many?

Ultimately, it's up to you which reality you choose to live in, just as it is up to me to choose my own reality. You can't get any more subjective than that!

CHAPTER 3
ON SUBJECTIVE REALITY

First off, let me start out by clarifying my terms. What I mean when I say that I Am the Ultimate Reality, I do not mean Dara Fogel, my ego-centric, vice-ridden, lousy little self. I mean that nameless part of me that existed before I was born into this realm of reality, and shall continue long after this personality is forgotten. What I am referring to is the eternal and (dare I say it?) most divine part of me – that fragment of Source that became embodied in this particular time-space nexus.

This seems to be where a lot of people get hung up about Subjective Reality. They mistake the Self for the self. They think the ego must provide all the answers, and they know intuitively that their limited egos don't have them. The Self that is the Ground of Being of Subjective Reality is not something that has to be made, as it was already created whole and perfect outside of time-space. Rather, it is something to connect to. It's existence is not dependent on what I as my ego-self do or say or think, instead, it is about whether or not I choose to be a part of that larger Self that is connected to Everything That Is.

If you are reading this, then you already are questioning the mainstream paradigm version of reality. Either you started noticing the editing fingerprints on your life (i.e: strange synchronicities, against-all-odds events, unexpected last-minute saves, etc.), or something knocked you out of your accustomed view of reality (i.e.: psychedelics, exposure to conscious material, spontaneous experiences, etc.). This would not interest you unless you were already on your way to waking up to Subjective Reality.

Since Subjective Reality is so... well... damned subjective, all I can really know is my own experience. But the ancients teach us "As Above, So Below. As Within, So Without," and experience has proven to me that this is true. Everything I experience is the perfect expression of my consciousness at that given moment. My ego-self may be agonizing and hating, but when I stop and truly observe myself, I always see that that which I am hating and agonizing over originates and ends in me. It is but my own thoughts that create my hell. Even when I am in pain, it is not necessarily the physical sensations that are so bad. Rather, it is what I tell myself - *my* interpretation of *my* experience - that makes any pain, physical or emotional, bearable or not. I know this from personal experience, not from something I read or someone told me.

Subjective Reality & Gnosticism

Subjective Reality (SR) is necessarily gnostic – that is, it is based in personal experience. You are never asked to take anything on faith in Subjective Reality. In fact, as the Microcosm of the Macrocosm, it is your job to explore your world and discover Truth for yourself. No one can give this to you, and if they could, you wouldn't want someone else's regurgitated Truth. If a second-hand truth would suffice, again, you would not be interested in learning more about SR.

But the self that we usually experience is the "little *s* self," not the vastness of the All Conscious Self. Unless we have a spontaneous experience, such as a Near Death Experience (NDE), or some kind of other Out of Body Experience (OBE) that jerks us into that other, larger plane of existence, you have to figure it out for yourself. You could say that the "big S Self" is like a Dreamer, and your "little s self" is a version of your "big S Self" inside the dream. You could also say that what you experience as your "small s self" is an avatar or game piece inside the context of the game, while the "big S Self" is the Player. When we are thrown out of our habituated routes of consciousness, we can become aware of the "big S Self," The Dreamer, the Player.

Luckily, the clues are everywhere you look, in everything you touch, see, smell, hear and taste. But you have to choose to *recognize* the clues *as* clues, and then follow to see where they lead. Even if you are thrown into that other state by a NDE or OBE, like I was, you still have to choose how you will interpret your experience and how you will respond. And you have to keep choosing, lest you revert to the Default Reality you started out with.

But again, our larger Self is generous, as He/She/It is always as close as your own heartbeat. The trick is to quit beating up on yourself with your thoughts or distracting yourself long enough to make and maintain conscious contact. You are not asked to trust anyone but yourself. You are not asked to listen to anyone's advice (including mine), but instead are always pointed back towards your own counsel.

Some find this immensely freeing. I did, as I never could quite swallow any of the world religions' teachings – until I encountered Hinduism and Gnosticism. These traditions encouraged me to explore my experiences and provided an invaluable guide and framework for me to develop in a balanced way.

(Note: if you are interested in knowing more about my own awakening experiences, check out my novel, ***The Impossible Lover. Although it is fictionalized and placed in totally different circumstances and characters, I drew greatly from my own experiences for the descriptions of states of being and consciousness.)

But some find this appalling/frightening/bewildering. This is based on a lack of trust in yourself. If you can't trust yourself to know what is real, then, by default, you must rely on someone else's conception of reality and choose to adopt it as your own. But how do you know that those you have chosen to trust are truly trustworthy? What if those you take your reality cues from are not acting in your best interest?

Self Sabotage

In SR terms, this is Self Sabotage. Instead of trusting our own Inner Guidance, we look outside – but there really isn't any outside. It is like we are inside a holodeck that can only reflect back what images and experiences we program in. So the lower, limited, scared little s self creates these horrible fantasies, and puts them into the mouths of "authority figures" or other characters whose words we put high value on, effectively programming the holodeck to play that scenario, whether it's an illness, financial/career, or personal.

The unconscious mind then starts to repeat these stories, and goes about enacting them, often without our conscious awareness... but many times with our conscious awareness. For how many times have you done something knowing that it would come back and bite you in the butt, but you actually kind of wanted that butt-biting, in a weird sort of way. When you get four or five decades under your belt, you start to see these patterns.

Current science tells us that 95 -98% of our choices are actually unconscious. We are actually mostly running on knee-jerk reactions, and putting a rational justification gloss over them. For me, this is a whole lot scarier than the idea that SR is some sort of overblown egotism and self-indulgence. If most of what I do is unconscious, and there really is a real external reality and most of what everyone does is unconscious, driven by deep hidden emotions and personal agendas beyond anyone's control, then we are in big trouble!

But if I am a part of the Ultimate Ground of Being, then I have an active part to play. If all of this exists because of me, then I must be meant to participate in some meaningful fashion. In SR, we choose our own meaning, rather than just uncritically swallowing someone else's. That doesn't mean that my ego-self knows everything. *But it does mean that I have access to an Inner Self who does know and control everything.*

People freak out about SR because they think that they have to know and do everything. They think that what I call radical Epistemic Responsibility is something to be afraid of. But the truth is just the opposite: the consciousness that you think of as YOU is the one *being known and seen* by your Inner Self – that highest, purest and completest part of that swirling of potential energy that is you. Then, your job becomes keeping the little ego small s self out of the way of gumming up the works of the Inner Self that is your portal to All-That-Is. Your job isn't to micromanage the Universe; it is to recognize that you already *are* the Universe, and were before your puny ego ever came into existence.

Now, I like my SR with a chaser of Soft Determinism. This is a result of my direct experience. Your experience might inform you differently. That's ok in SR. (Steampunk, too. That's why I love it so!) You get to have your reality and I get to have mine, and we can hang out where they overlap. See: Intersubjective Agreement).

My experience was of a storyline outside of time. Without time, that means that all of the story exists at once and is complete, and therefore determined. (Again, for more detained descriptions, I refer you to my novel, The Impossible Lover.)

Of course, this brings up the inevitable question of morality and responsibility. SR is not against karma or cause and effect... necessarily. Karma and cause and effect can be transcended by intention and alignment, hence those miraculous last-minute saves, extraordinary coincidences and beating overwhelming odds that make up so much of our personal biographies and those stories we see in the media.

But, again, the ego is not the one who is or should be in charge. Even with the best of intentions, the little self is so encumbered by false beliefs and misperceptions that it should not be trusted as final arbiter of morality. And as G.I. Gurdjieff said, the average person's mind is so weak that he cannot "do" anything. Rather, he is being

13

done by everything. Recognition of this is the starting point.

But it all comes down to the simple choice: Who are you going to believe about what is real? If you have had an NDE or an OBE, you may not have that option. Then your choice is about follow-up – now that you know, what are you going to do with that knowledge?

Plato, Krishna, heck, even Wayne Dyer tell us that becoming aware of what you do is the first step on the path to Self-Mastery. I'll list a couple of easy exercises below for you to start to observe and make your own decisions about what approach to reality is realer. ☺

So this kind of smacks of religion, doesn't it?

I am asking you to accept my personal testimony as evidence that our inner work is much more important than our external/social lives. SR's subjective nature makes it impossible for me to discuss the topic except through my own experience. But I am in very good company in seriously discussing the topic. SR has gone through many different names through the ages. Subjective Reality is just the latest packaging of the same awareness found in the Bhagavad Gita, Plato, the Essenes, and Quantum Physics.

The more writing of fiction that I do, the more I realize how much this everyday reality is a fiction. As the Author of "the Story of Dara's Life" (hopefully, its real title is more profound), I have unlimited access to the plot structure, IF and only if I am willing to utilize it. Most of us don't. If my life is like a narrative story, then it is up to me to decide if I am playing the Protagonist or the Spear-Carrier in the Third Act who delivers a message and is never seen again. That is where Free Will comes in.

Authors of fiction have often related how a minor character in a story "took over" and became a main character. I think it's the same with us. We can allow others to motivate and manipulate us, or we can try to be more than what we have been. We can enlarge our part to rock star status, if we choose to embody it.

But, ultimately, YOU are the one doing the choosing. YOU are the one who is making a leap of faith, no matter what you decide. There is just as much evidence for a Subjective approach as there is for an Objective – more even. For quantum science even tells us that it is observation that is the determining factor in the universe we experience.

But nothing beats personal experience.

So I dare you – I double-dog dare you to look inside yourself and see what you find.

Exercises:

1) Self-Observation

Pay attention to how you talk to yourself. Particularly when you are emotional or frustrated. Try to "catch yourself in the moment." Do these exercises for a week and keep a journal to keep track of your observations. How do you treat yourself? What kind of language do you use? Who else do you treat this way?

2) Keep a Journal.

It helps a lot to record your thoughts and observations. It is especially helpful to go back and read later, when in a different mood and mindset to see how differently you feel with the passage of time and events.

3) Track coincidences, deja vus, unusually vivid or strange dreams, etc. You might be surprised at what you find over time.

CHAPTER 4
DEFINING THE SELF: A PRELIMINARY STUDY

(Author's Note: this essay was does not address Subjective Reality directly, but it does explore a variety of extant approaches to the self, laying the groundwork for deeper understanding. This essay was written while I was working on my doctorate, as the culmination of an independent study I did into the nature of the self.)

Views of the self are as numerous and varied as stars in the sky or grains of sand on the beaches. It is not unrealistic to say that there are as many theories of the self as there are people who have had thoughts about what it means to be an individual. But if we are to ever articulate an ethic founded in self-knowledge, a clear definition of the self is mandatory: for how can we even begin to fulfill the required mandate of self-knowledge if we don't even know what a "self" is to have knowledge of?

The need for a clear delineation of the self poses a unique and somewhat paradoxical problem. The study of the self and what it means to be a self is necessarily subjective and intimate. Any attempts to formulate an objective and universal definition of the self is limited from its inception, because as soon as the definer looks outside of his/her self, they are no longer discussing the self – they are necessarily discussing behavior. And I think it fairly safe to claim that observed behavior and experienced selfhood are two entirely different things. But reflection and self-reports are also questionable, as subjectivity is well known to cloud clear observation.

Another problem in getting a clear definition of the self is that the deep self is notoriously non-rational, all of our attempts to forge a rational articulation of the self cannot be complete, as aspects of the self will always exist beyond the ability of words to describe.

These limitations imposed by the nature of selfhood renders our accustomed philosophical tools of observation, reflection and logic somewhat ineffective, as none of these approaches can truly encompass the totality of what it is to be a self.

Yet, almost anyone asked would answer affirmative if asked if they possessed a self. But do they? How would we know? How could we prove the existence of a self in another person? Or demonstrate the lack of a self?

Like trying to grab fog, everyone can see the presence of a self, but no one can capture its essence. For as soon as we would try to objectify the self, we are confronted with our own subjective experience of the self. Any 'objective' description of the self immediately spurs reflection and self-observation in the hearer to verify the truth of the 'objective' claims against personal experience.

In the philosophy of mind, this is known as the problem of other minds – what proof do we have that others have an internal self, other than external behavior implying they have a self? Any attempts to formulate such an 'objective' description of the self is necessarily colored and perhaps skewed by the subjectivity of the self that does the formulating. It is a circular operation with no definite boundaries.

But these problems of defining of the self have not deterred thousands from making the attempt. From the dawn of recorded history people have tried to explain what it was to be a self, and what selfhood implies for the study of ethics (i.e.: being a self amongst other selves). Because of the sheer volume of literature on the topic of the self, a comprehensive and complete survey of all existent theories of the self is an impossible goal for this essay. However, there are some clear and influential views of the self that have been articulated.

Being a subjective self, myself, I have my own take on what it means to be/have a self and what this implies for both individuals and collective societies. As I cannot willfully divorce myself from my selfhood, my theory of self is necessarily drawn from personal experience and self-reflection. But I also incorporate the ideas of others when they seem well thought-out and reasonable. While I try to remain as objective and rational as I am able, the topic of the self will, no doubt, slip into the subjective and non-rational. I beg the indulgence of my readers as I endeavor to balance the outer with the inner, the objective with the subjective, observation with experience.

I begin my attempt to articulate a model of the self with a brief description of three major movements in the understanding of the self. This includes descriptions of theories of the self both ancient and modern, in which I will lay out defining features of the theories and show their relevance. I will draw some conclusions and implications for an ethic founded upon knowledge of the self, according to these views. Finally, I will finish by raising and answering foreseeable objections to this position.

Popular Approaches to the Self Through History

A) Classics – The Tripartite Soul

In the *Republic*, Plato attempts to answer the question "what is justice?" In my opinion, this is the fundamental problem of ethics, for justice is universally held as the ideal for social interaction and modeling. In Plato, the question of justice boils down to a question of the self. Plato spends ten books describing the ideal and theoretical relations of the self and society. As Plato tells us in Book II, the individual can be likened to the polis (city-state), in that the city embodies the same ideas and values as the individuals that constitute it. (*Republic*, Book II, 368d – 369a) By describing the differing types of relations within a city, Plato also describes what he takes to be the type of relations within an individual self.

In the end, justice is defined as a certain balance of internal relationships in both the city and the individual. (*Republic*, Book IV, 443c – e) To articulate this, Plato describes what has been called the "Tripartite Soul," in which the self is divided into three parts: 1) Reason; 2) Spirit/Will; and 3) the Desires or Appetites. These three parts of the soul correspond to three classes of society. Respectively, these are: 1) the Rulers (Philosopher-Kings); 2) the Guardians (the military class) and 3) the Craftsmen (everyone else).

Reason is held to be the highest part of the individual, as it is through the rational faculty that the self can grasp the ideals embodied in the forms. Reason is the controller and harmonizer of the other two parts.

The Spirit or Will is seen to be the faculty which allows us to choose and to apply ourselves in the face of hardship, but this part can become discouraged or obsessive and needs the guidance of reason.

The Desires are the bodily drives to maintain corporeal existence and to propagate the species, which can again usurp the just rule of reason if out of balance.

Each of these parts has it's own respective virtues and vices, strengths and weaknesses, which can be encouraged or suppressed at the choice of the rational self.

Justice in both the polis and the individual is then defined as:

"...with respect to what is within, and respect to what truly concerns him and his own. He [the just citizen] doesn't let each part in him mind other people's business or the three classes in the soul meddle with each other, but really sets his own house in good order and rules himself; he who arranges himself becomes his own friend, and harmonizes the three parts, exactly like three notes in a harmonic scale, lowest, highest and middle. And if there are some other parts in between, *he binds them together and becomes entirely one from many, moderate and harmonized. Then, and only then, he acts...*" (*Republic*, Book IV, 443d, emphasis added)

Plato claimed the foundation of personal and social action (AKA: ethics) is in the harmonization and balancing of the three distinct features found within each individual self. For my purposes, Plato's use of the term "soul" or "psyche" is analogous to my use of "the self." Both refer to the subjective experience of being, including the relations of that subjective being to the subjective beings of others.

In his description of the tripartite self, it is clear that Plato (via Socrates) is not referring to a conception of an everlasting soul. His description is of a pragmatic perception of the human psyche in action. For Plato, this much-desired harmony of the soul is achieved by letting each internal part control that which it is best suited by function to its control.

As Plato tells us in Book I of *the Republic*, a virtue is by definition the proper functioning of the thing in question. For a person, the proper function of the soul is justice. (Book I, 353a – e) For this reason, the just man is not attracted to vice or injustice, as the harmoniously balanced just man has no desire to upset his hard-won balance through lying, cheating or stealing. (*Republic*, Book IV, 442e – 443a) "The contemplation of all time and all being" undertaken by the just self makes corporeal desires and thrills dull by comparison. (*ibid.,* Book IV, 486a)

This description of Plato's view of the human psyche is necessarily rudimentary and truncated, as it is only meant to prepare the ground for the later explication of my theory of self. To further my task of preparing a historical foundation, I now leap over two millennia to a consideration of a modern view of the self.

B) Modern Selves – Egos and Archetypes

Sigmund Freud, the so-called father of psychoanalysis, like Plato, also divided the human psyche into three parts: the Ego, the Id, and the Superego. (Pals, p. 61) In Freud's system, the Id corresponds roughly to the desire (Appetitive) aspect of Plato's tripartite soul. Freud's Id represents the most basic part of the psyche, which is primarily concerned with bodily drives – food, sex, security.

The Ego represents the center of the will and judgment – that which strives to maintain a balance between the three parts of the psyche. As I understand it, Plato has no exact counterpart for the ego, although some ego functions seem to be fulfilled by Plato's Rational part of the soul.

The Ego is the conscious self, the face we show to the public, as well as the private self we are internally aware of. The ego is the part of the self that rationally chooses, communicates and registers reactions, but all of the ego's functions can be skewed or even controlled by either the Id or the Superego in dysfunction. The Id and Superego can also subtly influence the ego below the level of awareness, causing the ego to believe it is behaving rationally and objectively, while in reality it is being manipulated by unconscious forces.

Freud's Superego represents the internalized influences of others impinging upon the individual, such as a critical parent or teacher. Again, there is no direct correspondence between Plato's and Freud's systems, but it appears that at least some of the functions of the superego are also embodied in the reasoning part of the tripartite soul, as well as some that can be located in Plato's Spirited segment of the soul.

Freud's view of the self has been extremely influential upon Western countries and has become internalized by our culture and institutions. Although Freud does not apply his work to a larger body of ethics, no account of the modern conception of the self could be deemed adequate without some reference to Freud's groundbreaking theories.

Of greater interest to me, however, is the work of Freud's student, Carl Jung. While Jung accepted much of Freud's psychological framework and theoretical approach of the "talking cure," one area in which Jung profoundly differed from Freud is in the understanding of humanity's unconscious. Freud's treatment of the Id presents the psychic processes below the level of awareness as a snakepit of repressed desires, impulses and instincts. Jung took a more optimistic view of the self below conscious awareness.

Jung abandoned the more traditional triune model of the self for a simpler dyadic model. Instead of three competing parts of the soul, Jung hypothesized the existence of only two: 1) the Ego, similar to Freud's understanding of the rational, conscious self, and 2) the Unconscious, which is seen as more comprehensive and influential than either the Id or Superego.

Jung's Ego is the persona by which we present ourselves to the world, "meaning between our true selves and our environment, just as our physical clothing presents an image to those we meet. The ego is what we are and know about consciously." (*Shadow*, Johnson, p. 3 – 4) The other side of the Ego is the Unconscious, which contains over ninety percent of our psychological being.

The unconscious contains the snakepits of Freud's Id, renamed the Shadow, as well as a rich inner world populated by internal characters and functions which embody many psychological patterns called Archetypes.

The archetypes are "essential building blocks in the psychic structure of every man and woman. If something is archetypal, it is typical. Archetypes form the basis for instinctive, unlearned behavior patterns that are common to all mankind, and represent themselves in human consciousness in certain typical ways." (Sandford, p. 6 – 7) These Archetypes are both personal and shared. The personal archetypes are embodied as the Anima/Animus, or the contra-sexual image-ideal within each individual. The anima or animus is the locus of many motivating functions of self-image and sexual relations.

The shared archetypes are contained in what Jung called the Collective Unconscious. They are called 'collective' because the same images and functions appear in some form across all times and cultures, and hence seem to be universally human. The unconscious holds our drives, impulses and instincts, as well as our aspirations and inspirations. The Collective Unconscious can be said to contain both the highest and the lowest that humans are capable of.

Because so much of our selves remain in the Unconscious, the majority of our selves are unknown. "Most people confuse 'self-knowledge' with knowledge of their conscious ego personalities... but the ego knows only its own contents, not the unconscious and its contents... What is commonly call 'self-knowledge' is therefore a very limited knowledge, most of it dependent on social factors, of what goes on in the human psyche." (Jung, p. 14 – 15)

What we experience as an unique individual is actually informed and controlled by the movement of these universal archetypes below the surface of awareness. The suggestion is that the internal self is predicated upon the existence of an internalized community of shared psychic patterns.

Jung is primarily an Essentialist, as the 'True Self' is contained within the Unconscious, and must be recovered and revealed through the intentional stripping away of emotional accretions and defense mechanisms.

These components (Archetypes) in the psyche compete for control and energy unless they are made conscious. Through a creative interactive process within the psyche called Active Imagination, in which internal questions and relations are investigated subjectively, bringing unconscious material into awareness. This process uses art, self-expression, imagination and ritual to give voice to and to dialogue with the internal characterizations of the archetypes.

Like Plato and Freud, Jung sought harmony within the warring parts of the self. But unlike Plato and Freud's subjugation of the unconscious to the rational or the ego, Jung's self-actualization consists of bringing more and more unconscious material into awareness and the conscious integration of this material into the self-consciousness. In Jung's view, the achievement of integration leads to balanced and harmonious social/interpersonal relations.

As I see it, Jung's view of the self offers three main advantages over the tripartite views of Plato and Freud:

1) Simplicity – only two segments of the self are posited, in accord with Ockham's Razor, although the balance of conscious and unconscious is not made any easier by the subsuming of elements of id and superego into the unconscious;

2) The Hope for Improvement/redemption as unconscious processes are absorbed into the consciousness through active imagination or other therapeutic techniques;

3) Compassion and Stability - Jung's model is more equitable and maintainable, in my opinion, than either Plato's or Freud's, as both of Jung's predecessors rely on a 'Dominator' model of the psyche, in which the unconscious forces must be held under tight control by reason or the ego. In Jung's version, increased awareness performs this function by integrating the splintered elements of the self.

Although Freud's 'talking cure' was also intended to bring unconscious elements into awareness, Freud limited his techniques to only the treatment of psychological pathologies. Jung used his techniques to bring about self-transformation and expanded awareness to everyman, as the means to achieve psycho-spiritual growth or self-actualization.

While Plato indicates that the reasoning part of the psyche can be educated through philosophy to harmonize with the other two parts, Jung claims that the struggle between the conscious and unconscious is part of a larger cycle of unfolding awareness of self and universe. This implies that the self is in a state of perpetual growth, giving hope for improved future prospects of increased consciousness, as increased awareness leads to improved communication and interaction with both self and others. The two parts of the self are to be brought together and honored as fundamental components of a wondrous whole.

In Plato and Jung, the spiritual seeker is justified in pursuing the intangible balance of inner harmony and the higher perceptions that brings, but Freud's focus on pathology precludes the use of his model for purposes other than seeking effective psychological function. For Freud, psychology was a medical discipline with the purpose of curing disease, not for self-exploration.

All three of these models tend to have a bias of elitism. For Plato, only those with the leisure to practice philosophy had any hope for achieving the delicate balance of the soul he calls justice. For Freud and Jung, only those with the resources and leisure to embark on lengthy psychoanalysis could hope to achieve mental health or self-actualization.

But of these two, Jung's system is more creative and less constrained by the therapist-patient relationship than Freud's system. While Freud's technique depends heavily on therapeutic sessions, Jung's technique is more accessible to the would-be self-actualizer. Through a multitude of excellent books (by Jung and his many followers) and through self-exploration in active imagination, an individual can begin to do "inner work" alone, without mortgaging the house to go into therapy, although a certain level of education and leisure is required in order to read, understand and apply Jung's teachings.

Social Constructivism and Biological Determinism

Social Constructivism is the position held in favor by current social science. It holds that an examination of social institutions and structures reveal a functional explanation of social roles apart from any contextual or subjective meaning. The individual is seen as shaped and constituted by the social roles he/she fulfills. (Rosenberg, p. 101-102)

This view is called "The Blank Slate" by MIT psychology professor Steven Pinker, and is contrasted by him to a biological-genetic basis for understanding the human psyche. The Social Constructivist position (Pinker's Blank Slate) holds that the effects of culture are what shapes an individual, lending features and distinction to an otherwise undifferentiated psyche. The Social Constructivists are in good company in this view of the lack of an essential human nature. Also holding this view are the influential philosophers, Descartes and Rousseau, who believed that the human psyche is fashioned primarily by external social forces.

More recent philosophers like Charles Taylor and Michael Sandel have espoused a Social Constructivist view of the self. For Taylor, the self is to be understood as having developed through the historical mediation of social institutions that he calls Frameworks or Orientations. Taylor asserts that we gain our sense of identity from sources both universal and individual, complex and many-layered. (*Sources*, Taylor, p. 29)

To define the self is to identify with Frameworks that provide a structure of meaning by giving standards for distinctions and evaluations. (Sources, Taylor, p.30) But these Frameworks are inherited, not created, as they exist prior to being chosen by an individual. We might be tempted to hear echoes of Jung's archetypes in Taylor's Frameworks were it not for a critical distinction which sets them opposite: In Taylor's view, the self is both molded by and is the medium of inherited social institutions (Frameworks) that are imposed upon the individual by external sources.

These Frameworks are accepted and internalized by the individual, imparting meaning and an orientation to experience. The emphasis is on the relation to these external Frameworks as the primary 'sources of the self' of Taylor's book of the same name. In Jung's approach, the self is the center of focus, with the Archetypes being internal sources of meaning and value, mediated through the Collective Unconscious.

Taylor offers external historic frameworks as a remedy to the three ailments of modern culture, which he identifies as: 1) Individualism; 2) the Disenchantment of the World; and 3) the Political Consequences of the first two malaises.

To Taylor, individualism, while offering a new autonomy to individuals, also entails the loss of traditional moral horizons that delineated and gave meaning to experience.

The Disenchantment of the World refers to the loss of cosmic order and higher purpose once imparted by historic institutions. This loss of purpose is linked to a narrowing of vision caused by egoism and self-centeredness.

Crucial to the success of this disenchantment is the rise of Instrumental Reasoning, in which rationality is focused on maximizing efficiency and profits. In Instrumental Reasoning, others are seen as means to our ends, human life is devalued by impersonal institutions, and science and technology is glorified in the worship and hope of the 'technological fix.'

This pragmatic modern rationalism differs from the Platonic model by emphasizing the enhancement of ordinary life, rather than focusing on abstract conceptual excellence. The political fallout of Individualism and Instrumental Reasoning is the loss of freedom due to the imposition of instrumental reasoning. As self-absorbed citizens fail to participate in government, soft despotism is given a foothold.

Without civic participation, individuals face monolithic institutions alone, further discouraging participation and alienating them from the political sphere. Without this, we are in danger of losing our ability to control our political destinies. (*Authenticity*, Taylor, p. 2 – 10)

For Taylor, meaning is created through connection to others. He asserts that an individual's values and choices are shaped by culture and caste, and cannot be totally self-generated, as Jung's collective unconscious could be construed to be. (*Authenticity*, Taylor, p. 47) Taylor links self-discovery to creative-artistic self-expression, but limits individual originality only to those creations which enhance social values. It is through immersion in the group traditions that the individual finds the fulfillment of his/her self.

There is much good to be found in Taylor, especially in his diagnosis of the 'Malaises of Modernity,' but I do not agree with the Social Constructivist view of a self entirely fashioned by culture and institution. The selfish egotism identified by Taylor is certainly a problem prevalent in our culture, but Jung would diagnose this condition as one of alienation from the true self, not at all a goal to be striven for, as Taylor seems to want to claim.

At the opposite spectrum of the approaches to understand the self is the Cognitive view of the self. In the Cognitive camp, the self is seen as the result of brain processes. The faculties of mind are believed to have evolved in response to conditions in the environments of our ancestors.

These faculties are characterized as modules in the mind, usually corresponding to specific locales in the geography of the human brain. The self or soul is seen as the interaction of these modules. Our selves are, in large part, determined by our genetic inheritance.

It is undeniable that many personality traits are inherited, as science continues to discover the physical processes by which this occurs. To his credit, Pinker does acknowledge some external input, in that certain faculties (such as language) do not develop unless the individual is provided a potential-enriched environment. But to the cognitive psychologist, the individual self is still determined and constrained by forces outside his/her conscious control.

And, like Freud, the exercise of Cognitive Therapy is limited to the correction of pathologies, not self-actualization or exploration. The Cognitive view also falls prey to Taylor's malaise, as the values and relations of the self are reduced to biological processes, devoid of significance and higher purpose. Like Freud, the Cognitive Psychology approach utilizes and glorifies Instrumental Reasoning, and thus is prone to all the political and moral devolution's identified by Taylor.

The Cognitive view of the self as multiple modules of different mental faculties returns us once again to a view of a splintered self. In the Cognitive schema, a module or group of modules act as a 'central executive,' coordinating and controlling the other competing modules. Like Freud, the Cognitive view is a contentious model, and the internal conflict is reflected in social conflict. But like Plato, the module responsible for rational thought is considered superior to the other modules.

By now, it should be apparent that I am biased in favor of the Jungian view of the self. It has the virtue of having both simplicity and depth. While positing only two divisions of the self, it accounts for the multiplicity of drives, instincts and aspirations, while affording the self not only creativity (like Taylor), but also spirituality – something conspicuously lacking in most of the other models thus discussed.

I included the sometimes lengthy descriptions of these other systems because I believe that each of them has something vital to contribute to a holistic understanding of the self. From Plato, we get the idea of the self as an internal relation. From Freud, we get the concept of unconscious processes requiring consciousness. From Jung, we have the enhanced collective unconscious and the archetypes. Social constructivism gives us a sense of the ethical relations and connection to larger contexts, while cognitive psychology allows us to explore the connections between physical processes and personal experience.

Now I shall turn my focus to some less conventional ways of viewing the self.

Nonconventional Approaches to the Self: The Evolution of Consciousness and Human Biocomputers

Before he became a cultural icon, Timothy Leary was a serious researcher of consciousness. Leary posits the existence of eight levels (or circuits) of development in the human psyche, ranging from infancy (Level 1 – Bio-survival) through post-biological development (Circuit 8). Leary claims that the majority of humanity has only evolved to the fourth circuit (adolescence, industrialization and hive socialization), and is striving to attain the fifth circuit, which is characterized as "culture-free, hive-free, gravity-free and hedonic." (Leary, *Info-psychology*, p. 75)

A privileged few have reached the sixth circuit, called the neuro-electric or Einsteinian circuit, in which humanity learns how to take control of its own brain and can fabricate reality at will. In Leary's system, the seventh and eighth circuits are post-human, as mankind will have evolved into a different form by the time we achieve these developmental levels.

Through yoga, ritual and the judicious use of entheogens, Leary claims that humanity is now responsible for its own conscious evolution. The view here is that certain states of consciousness can activate dormant elements in human DNA, causing evolutionary changes within that individual and within humanity as a whole.

Leary's system is much more intricate than I have the space to describe, as each circuit has three stages, for a total of twenty-four possible stages of consciousness. Leary's ultimate goal is to activate all twenty-four stages of the eight circuits of attain what he calls "Metaphysiological Fusion."

Obviously, such an advanced level of activation is far beyond our own, and is described as "the linkage of the universe of everything with the void of everything" through the integration and manipulation of atomic-nuclear signals. (Leary, *Info-psychology*, p. 132 – 133)

Leary also links his system to the traditional metaphysical/alchemical keys of astrology and the tarot, and throws in a little I Ching to keep it balanced. The salient points of Leary to my own system are the concepts of conscious evolution and taking responsibility of our own nervous systems.

A colleague and fellow consciousness explorer with Leary is John Lilly. Lilly pioneered work in altered states of consciousness through isolation tanks, exploring the depths of individual consciousness. Lilly adopts a computational model of mind in assuming the human brain to "be an immense Biocomputer." (*Metaprogramming*, Lilly, p.3) Lilly holds that our behavioral, emotional and spiritual aspects are programs running on the Biocomputer, and are therefore mostly unconscious.

These programs often compete for expression and resources (similar to our historic and contemporary models explored in the last section). An emotional-behavioral program can be instantly activated by a multitude of stimuli. In order to achieve harmony/balance/integration, we must become 'Metaprogrammers' and rewrite or even delete programs that are no longer useful or are damaged. Like Leary, Lilly used multiple techniques to reach the level of consciousness at which Metaprogramming becomes accessible. (Lilly, *Metaprogramming*, p. 9)

For the purposes of Metaprogramming, Lilly separates the self into two aspects: 1) the Observer – the self-aware part that watches the self, and 2) the Operator – which is the doing-participation aspect of the self. (Lilly, *Self*, p. 89) The whole self is called the "Observer-Operator."

The self, as observer-operator, is immersed in its own internal reality, even when actively engaged in activities in external reality. The observer-operator can only perceive external reality through the lens of its own internal reality.

Lilly was the first to coin and describes what he calls "Consensus Reality," which is defined as "that set of beliefs/assumptions/postulates/interpretations/simulations that each of us is given/absorbs that are said to be real/true in our culture/society/family/school etc. Consensus Reality is that which is agreed to be real/true... [through] one collection or another of simulations of internal reality/external reality with which one agrees/disagrees. A large fraction of our most securely held sacred beliefs is in the consensus group of simulations of reality." (Lilly, *Self*, p. 90) This is essentially the same thing as Intersubjective Agreement.

All beliefs and personality traits are seen as programs open to reprogramming and tweaking. As such, reality itself as we experience it is up for grabs. Lilly suggests the creation of a 'Metabelief Operator' who perfects the belief programs responsible for creating realities, both internal and external. "Thus a metabelief operator is a concept/function/agent that operates on, transforms, introduces changes into belief systems." (Lilly, Self, p. 90 – 91)

Using the Metabelief Operator and Metaprogramming techniques, we can explore/transform our Biocomputer, programming it to perceive beyond the accustomed ruts of Consensus Reality. In his later years, Lilly turned to a Fourth Way School (ala Gurdjieff) as a means to further develop self-observational detachment from the confines of his own internal reality.

From Leary, we get a sense of cosmic-biological urgency to transform our low level of conflicted consciousness, and from Lilly, we get detailed instructions on how to consciously manipulate our realities, internal and external. Leary would say that Jung's Archetypes are symbolic representations of the twenty-four levels of the Eight-Circuit Brain. Lilly would call the Archetypes programs running in the Biocomputer, projected onto Consensus Reality.

A Mix-and-Match Self

Up until the mid-twentieth century, models of the self were generally dual or tripartite models, but later twentieth century models were more willing to allow a greater complexity to the human psyche.

We began with the three-part models of Plato and Freud, then moved to the dual model of Jung. Although Jung only posited two fundamental parts of the psyche, his construal of the unconscious was so configured as to allow a multiplicity of functions under the single rubric of the Collective Unconscious and their resident Archetypes.

The Social Constructivist view permitted an unlimited number of modules to perform the many functions of the psyche, with none assuming primacy, but rather allowed for them all or for coalitions of modules to come together, as well as allowing advances in brain physiology to play a part.

Leary's Eight-Circuit Brain allows a more organized reading of the modular brain, while including the idea of individual psychic growth.

Lilly's Metaprogramming gives us a specific technique for harnessing the various parts of the self, be they three or three thousand.

All of the approaches reviewed in this essay, from Plato to Social Cognitive, rely upon an ultimate integration and harmonization of the multiple parts of the self in order to become a balanced self. Lilly's approach gives us a systematic way to achieve the integrations required, while the other systems seem more haphazard in their means of integration. So in the end, a picture of the self emerges that consists of many parts that somehow must be brought into some sort of alignment.

The various approaches have differing theories of the origins of the multi-faceted self – the some of them (Plato, Jung, Leary) seem to imply that these parts of the self are essential to human nature and self-generated; while the Social Constructivist position (Taylor) holds that these parts are created through social process.

Sitting on the fence are Pinker and Lilly, both of whom seem to incorporate elements of both the essentialism of Plato and company, while still allowing room for the interaction of social processes to impact and shape the emergence of selves.

I believe all of these positions have something to contribute. I most closely agree with Pinker and Lilly, in that I agree that many things in the psyche are biologically and socially determined, but I want to allow for Jungian features through Lilly's model of multiple programs.

Lilly's model of the Biocomputer is very useful, but dry, in that the description of mental programs lack content. Jung remedies this lack with the rich field of Archetypes to give depth and color to the internal programs. So, armed with the creativity of Jung and with the organization of Lilly, I believe that a multi-faceted self emerges who can shape and construct their own reality. Leary shows us a self in progress, and from Plato, we must assume the responsibility for the necessary harmonization of self-completion.

We end up with a representation of the self that must develop itself to integration through its own efforts. This places a great deal of responsibility upon both individuals and the society, not only to take the self into hand (so to speak), but also to provide the guidance and conditions for this necessary self-completion.

An actualized and harmonized self will lead to greater social harmony and cohesion if carried to a cultural and global scale. But our culture does not yet recognize these self-needs and does not give assistance or guidance to self-integration. To implement an ethics based on this model would require a major awakening of personal and social responsibility.

Objections and Responses

1)   The first most obvious objection is that this seems like a mishmash of approaches. And this criticism is correct – I have not offered single a comprehensive view, but rather have picked and chosen certain aspects of each that I find appealing. This is a preliminary articulation of my emerging position and will require more work to uncover all the logical and ethical implications. But I believe it is a good start.

2)   The next objection is the massive change in cultural consciousness required if we are to adopt this model of self-completion. It seems unlikely and impractical to expect this model to be adopted any time soon.

Difficulty in implementation is not necessarily a reason to not try. If the human race is ever to overcome our tendencies to live down to our lowest impulses, and instead to realize our highest potentials, we must accept responsibility for our selves, as well as for the consequences of our beliefs.

If the Social Constructivist view is correct (and I believe that it is, in part), then we are responsible for providing social and educational environments which will encourage individuals towards greater integration and harmony. Currently, our culture is a hodge-podge mixture of influences and the development of the self is left up to whatever forces, inner or outer, come to bear, shaping the self without reference to the achievement of harmony. I advocate a consciousness of the development of the self, and an awareness of the influences both internal and external.

3) An implemented program of self-development (if imposed by the government or social serves) is extremely prone to abuses, leading to mind control and mental tyranny. An emerging self would be made vulnerable to the whim of the system, which could be used to warp the selves into slaves or politically programmed.

The potential for abuse of this model renders it unusable for governmental or bureaucratic use. Individuals must be encouraged to seek and explore their own inner natures. The arts and education are ideal venues for this approach, but it cannot be enforced from the top down. It must be self-chosen in order to be consistent.

4) A model of the self is not really necessary. We have gotten to this far without a single model, so why would we need one now?

The increasing world population is causing a massive growth in multiculturalism, leading many to adopt a position of ethical relativism and ego-centrism. It is often argued that the world is becoming a more dangerous and frightening place, especially in the wake of global terrorism and war. A model of self-development could help to promote greater peace and cooperation in the world. If the world is populated with integrated individuals who are at peace with themselves, perhaps it would become harder to get violence and war started.

5) The final glaring problem with what I have described is that I have not yet shown how the individual is intimately connected to everyone else and the whole planet. This gets into the realm of

Subjective Reality – and that's another topic...

CHAPTER 5
EXPLORING CONSCIOUSNESS

"In the province of the mind, what one believes to be true is true or becomes true, within certain limits to be found experientially and experimentally. These limits are further beliefs to be transcended. In the mind, there are no limits."

-John C. Lilly, MD.

Perhaps it is hubris to think that humanity carries within its mind the capacity to become as gods. Or perhaps it is an intuition of humanity's true nature. Who can say for sure? And yet, throughout the length of recorded history, there have always been those willing to sacrifice the benefits and comforts of the externally focused life to reach for the possibility of an inner existence unbounded by material considerations and limitations.

Is it only wishful thinking or can it be the emergence of a new level of being? Over three decades ago, two renegade scientists each undertook to explore possible answers to these questions. Their discoveries, while answering some questions, have served to open other larger questions concerning the purpose and destiny of humanity.

In 1872, Charles Darwin forever changed the way Western culture looks at life on this planet. Instead of a static creation, we now perceive an evolving universe, staggeringly old, which has tried on and discarded countless forms, each more complex and integrated than the last, in its manifestation of untold lifeforms. In the study of primates, we see the evolutionary footprints of humanity and observe the social complexities of a highly evolved mammalian mind.

But as clever as apes can be, humans are still a quantum leap beyond. Anthropology has searched unsuccessfully for decades for a "missing link" to connect humans to their primal ancestors. Indeed, evolutionary biologists such as Stephen Jay Gould are now positing a theory of "punctuated evolution," in which advances occur in leaps and spurts, not always the slow increments assumed by Darwin, to explain the gaps in the evolutionary record.

Just as humanity is a leap beyond primates, what if humanity is now poised on the verge of another quantum leap? But what if this new level of being must be attained individually and voluntarily?

Many have held this position throughout recorded history, first in the fields of religion (as evidenced in faiths like Hinduism and all schools of mysticism in general) and more recently by a few renegade scientists and thinkers. These latter-day Gnostics have been willing to risk ridicule and professional ostracization in order to pursue what they believed was a pearl of great price- to be freed of the shackles of physicalism and to discover raw being.

What exactly were they seeking? This essay seeks to explore possible explanations of these supposed states through the eyes of two of the foremost researchers in this issue. But first, some clarification of what state these researchers were searching for.

Cosmic Consciousness

Back in 1901, a leading Canadian psychiatrist named Richard

Maurice Bucke, MD., attempted to define what he termed Cosmic Consciousness. For all intents and purposes, we shall use his definition of transcendental states.

"Cosmic Consciousness, then, is a higher form of consciousness than that possessed by the ordinary man. The prime characteristic of cosmic consciousness is, as its name implies, a consciousness of the cosmos, that is of the life and order of the universe. Along with the consciousness of the cosmos there occurs an intellectual enlightenment or illumination which alone would place the individual on a new plane of existence - would make him almost a member of a new species. To this is added a state of moral exaltation, an indescribable feeling of elevation, elation and joyousness, and a quickening of the moral sense, which is fully as striking and more important both to the individual and to the race than is the enhanced intellectual power. With these come, what may be called, a sense of immortality, a consciousness of eternal life, not a conviction that he shall have this, but the consciousness that he has it already... [O]ur descendants will sooner or later reach, as a race, the condition of cosmic consciousness, just as, long ago, our ancestors passed from simple to self consciousness." (Bucke, 1901)

Bucke and many others assert that this state is not only achievable, but is even becoming increasingly common, as evolutionary forces continue apace.

It can be argued that history has already been positively impacted by the occurrence of this higher level of awareness through the personages of so-called "enlightened" religious avatars, such as Gautama Buddha, Moses, Jesus Christ and Mohammed, who all served to provide a much needed ethos and vision to not only their own generation, but for ages to come. Whatever mental states these individuals experienced, the force of it prompted them to abandon self-interest to pursue a higher ideal and imparted to them the capacity to inspire others to greater morality. Indeed, the force of their vision is still very much alive today in the many world religions which developed in the wake of these impactful individuals.

Although the actual experience of cosmic consciousness may only be for a few seconds, its potency is reportedly sufficient to forever change the recipient. Philosopher and mathematician, Blaise Pascal, recorded his own moment of personal revelation in 1654, and carried a testimonial of it, the *Memorial*) sewn into the lining of his jacket for the rest of his life. None can deny his contributions to the fields of calculus and philosophy.

Dante, Francis Bacon, Spinoza, William Blake, Walt Whitman, Swedenborg, Emerson, Thoreau and Wordsworth have variously been cited as having had experienced this fleeting illumination, which afterwards marked their works and lives. The original inspiration of these few has widely affected culture and morality, both within and outside of religious contexts. The aesthetic and ethical impact of this awareness is undeniable in Eastern cultures as well as in the West.

The subjectivity of Eastern cultures embraced this consciousness and actively sought to cultivate it, as in the meditational practices of Buddhist and Hindu yoga and the sacred dances of Sufism. In the West, instances of transcendental states occurred within the religious tradition (such as in the case of St. Theresa of Avila), but generally were not seen as an achievable goal. Eventually the pursuit of transcendental states was geerally abandoned in favor of the promise of science and technology. Yet, these states continually appeared sporadically among those few thinkers willing to forsake practicality for the possibility of an intangible.

In the last fifty years, the lure of transcendental states once again emerged as an underground current, surfacing here, then disappearing to resurface elsewhere. In the ferment of the 1960's, encouraged by the new advances in the fields of biology, neurology and psychology, a small number of scientists again raised the question of the value and relevance of transcendental states and sought to use their professional training to discover and explore them.

The names of many of these intrepid explorers of subjective mind impacted the drug culture of the '60's and '70's, such as Timothy Leary and Richard Alpert (a.k.a. Ram Das). Because of the hysteria and hype of that era, much of the substantive works in subjective mind research was either dismissed or driven underground, as recreational use of psychoactive drugs undermined the creditability of the researchers. Yet, some very interesting theories came out of those wild years, only to be ignored. Yet, it was some of the brightest minds of that generation who glimpsed beyond and dared to report their findings.

The most infamous of these inner travelers was Timothy Leary. Unfortunately, his flamboyant personality eclipsed much of his research at Harvard. Lesser known and much more respected in his field is John C. Lilly, MD., who researched at John Hopkins Medical Center in neurology, isolation research and later, interspecies communications with dolphins.

Both of these scientists adopted something of a machine functionalist stance, using a computational model of mind, but eventually abandoned materialist monism in favor of a sort of idealism that I call Subjective Reality. Both began to explore subjective states, at first, just to see what was there, recapitulating Descartes' *cogito*. But they were equipped with tools Descartes never imagined - that being the fruits of over three centuries of scientific inquiry and well-funded laboratories.

Both Leary and Lilly, working independently of one another, came to remarkably similar conclusions, though from different angles. The use of computational models and programmability inevitably led to theories of pro-active programming for transcendental states. Experimentation with hallucinogens had whetted their appetites for the real thing.

The Eight-Circuit Brain and the Evolution of Consciousness

In his more serious works, Leary posits twenty-four levels of awareness, ranging from the simplest bio-survival (marine) stages to the most complex, what he termed "cyber-nano-tech piloting."

These twenty-four levels can be sub-divided into eight larger groupings, that cover historical/evolutionary periods from invertebrate through post-quantum evolution, which he called "circuits." These eight circuits can be further divided into two parts, in which the first twelve are characterized as terrestrial, collective and mechanical, while the latter twelve stages are characterized as post-terrestrial, cyber-quantum stages. (3)

In the first twelve stages, the individual is seen as evolving up from proto-neucletic slime up through and including Homo Sapiens. Humans are seen as developing within the context of the social collective, which conditions and programs individuals according to the dominant culture.

Yet contained within that individual's being, Leary claims, is a pre-programmed genetic blueprint set to unfold once certain internal and external conditions are met. Once humanity passes a certain level of individual biological evolution (the fourth circuit), then other internal programs kick in to further individuate the consciousness to such a degree that, given enough time, Leary asserts that humanity will eventually have conscious control of the quantum level, not only of their own bodies, but also of physical reality. Leary proposed the marriage of an enlightened consciousness with advanced technology for the realization of humanities' possible potential.

"Since the neurological 60's we have seen an efflorescence of consumer sensuality and body interest. Massage, sensory awakening, yoga, martial arts, diet, health-food fads, erotic performance. The 'new hedonics' is a manifestation of the first beginnings of circuit five Zen consciousness." (Leary, 1993)

For Leary, the triggering causal factor of this new development was the discovery of neuro-somatic drugs. The explosive use of drugs on the 60's and 70's provided millions with the neurological impetus to evolve, but their urges were stymied by the lack of cultural and technological vehicles with which to do so. The result has been "grounded butterflies, neurologically ready, but technologically unprepared for flight. Instead of being hailed as harmless heralds of a mutation to come, they were predictably derogated and forced underground." (Leary, 1993)

Like many materialists, Leary agrees that the nervous system determines every aspect of human reality. Where he departs from the philosophical beaten path is in his claims of conscious subjective control of the nervous system and its development. To Leary, through conscious manipulation, DNA can be used to receive, integrate and transmit information at the genetic and quantum levels.

Leary admits that the majority of humanity is not yet at a level where they can conceive of what he terms "quantum intelligence." But, he claims that logic forces the conclusion of a probablist higher form of intelligence governing the force of evolution, when faced with the alternative explanations for the presence of intelligent life on earth. The only other cosmological alternatives offered currently are either "accidental, haphazard clustering of proteins and carbohydrates triggered by lightning bolts in pre-Cambrian slime leaving 'man' the highest dismal form of a ruthless survival battle, or anthropomorphized police-court Jehovahs of monotheism."(Leary, 1989)

Leary's system goes beyond existing mainstream models of mind, but easily accommodates them within the flexible developmental model of twenty-four levels, hence the behaviorism of Skinner would find its place in the third circuit of Symbolic Tool stage, and functionalism finds its slot in the fourth Industrial circuit.

Leary claims that the process of evolution utilizes a relentless continuity in the scheduling of mutations. Yet, the examination of genetic mutations in relation to consciousness has been and still is taboo. Leary urges us to consider the implications of future mutations of humanity in the face of an accelerated pace of evolution due to technological interference and interaction. The sooner we take personal responsibility for our own evolution, the better we can manifest it.

John Lilly and Meta-Programming of the Human Bio-Computer

John Lilly, by contrast to Leary's extravagance, remained securely ensconced in academia, doing ground-breaking work in biophysics and human-dolphin relations. He was also a leading authority on states of solitude, isolation and confinement and their psychological effects.

Lilly asserts that all humans are programmed bio-computers, thus, like Leary, taking something of a machine functionalist stance. As such, we are unable to escape our natures as programmable entities.

Most of the programs we live by are built in, set from birth and limited in number. Other programs arise culturally as the cerebral cortex grew in size and complexity. Programs unrelated to survival and reproduction emerged over time, allowing new levels of programs to emerge, using the older more basic programs as an underlying context.

Eventually, according to Lilly's theory, the cerebral cortex developed as a higher-level computer, capable of controlling and inhibiting the lower-level built in programs. It is here, Lilly claims, that learning and the use of symbols originated. Once a certain critical size and complexity of the cerebral cortex was achieved through millennia of evolution, language and its consequences emerged. (Lilly, 1968)

Lilly suggests that it is possible to "metaprogram the human bio-computer." By this, he means a central control system which controls hundreds of thousands of programs operating in parallel simultaneously. (Lilly, 1968) Lilly posits that out of the multiple programs and metaprograms in an well-ordered bio-computer, at least one metaprogram emerges as the critical control for interacting with and on other programs, and which is commonly labeled "I" or the self.

In Lilly's model, self-development is to centralize control of one's individual bio-computer into a single self-metaprogrammer, which coordinates and subordinates other programs and metaprograms under a single administration metaprogram, thus unifying the sometimes conflictual subordinate programs in the achievement of new levels of metaprogramming and operations. This is identical to the teachings of G.I. Gurdjieff and Fourth Way Schools, and accounts for why Lilly in his later years sought out training in the Fourth Way.

Above the individual level of bio-computers may exist an executive metaprogrammer(s), which Lilly calls the Supraself Metaprogram. This concept has been variously labeled "God, the creator, the Starmaker," etc. by bio-computers at different levels of operation and programming. (Lilly, 1972)

Lilly claims this unification of metaprograms is not only possible, but is actually the next evolutionary step for humanity. This property of unification, then, serves to create and manipulate a model of the universe within the self, which can be varied appropriately to match the real universe as necessary.

Lilly cautions us, however, not to become overly attached to any model of the universe, as it may not satisfactorily reflect the true states of reality, and feelings of awe, certainty, reverence and sacredness (such as Bucke described) are merely further programs that can be manipulated and thus not reliable measures of how well the current model matches reality. Humanity has a well-known disposition to self-delusion and wish-fulfillment, and would-be metaprogrammers must beware becoming entrapped inside their own models.

Lilly's main area of interest is that of self-metaprogramming, which is initiated consciously and then operates below the threshold of awareness. This concept is similar to suggestibility, but is more inclusive, as it also involves sources, inputs, outputs and central processes, as well as the resultant behavior. (Lilly, 1968)

Certain chemical substances have the effect of making the bio-computer more susceptible to reprogramming and metaprogramming and can be used advantageously to modify existing programs or to create new ones. But, he claims, not all programs are revisable, such as some necessary for survival or others created during emergencies in the early growth period of the bio-computer. Also, personal prioritization of programs can limit or metaprogram other programs, as some programs are ascribed more value than others.

In general, the "consciousness program" can be expanded or contracted within certain limits, but on the whole, major systems or metaprograms and programs compete for available circuitry and realization. Thus the expansion of one program decreases the available space for other programs.

Lilly advocates the use of various techniques and methods to free up the available circuitry from external excitation programs so that more resources can be devoted to internal cognitive reality and its analysis. To achieve this, Lilly experimented with various forms of yoga, isolation tanks and psychoactive drugs. In this, he cautions against being seduced by the potential for pleasure in these states, as the internal reality experienced is postulated by the expectations of the individual bio-computer and can be misleading.

Through the use of these and other possible undiscovered techniques, bio-computers can manipulate and overcome limits on operations caused by incomplete or incorrect programming. Towards this end, in his later works, Lilly introduces a schema of ten levels of structures in the human bio-computer, ranging from the external reality (including the body and brain) on the lowest level, up through the structure, programming and metaprogramming of the ego, self and essence, respectively, culminating in the unknown. (Lilly, 1972)

To "clean up" one's bio-computer, Lilly claims that both physical as well as mental exercises are necessary. The ultimate goal of all this inner rigor and exploration is to join a supraself network of conscious creators, (much as is described by Olaf Stapledon in his novel, the Starmaker) which Lilly believes to be the ultimate destination of human consciousness.

Evaluation

Both of these authors are dealing with an issue that is highly subjective and does not lend itself readily to external verification. Yet both offer arguments that seem reasonable within the contexts of their theories.

As Leary claims, there is no reason to believe that humanity's current level of development is the penultimate, and future mutations are always a possibility. However, there is little to no objective evidence of the existence of neural circuits beyond the fifth (the level now achieved by humanity). Some of Leary's more radical claims about extraterrestrial intelligence and space migration may or may not be justified, but his claim that humanity must now take an active part in our own evolution does seem to be at least partially borne out.

With the explosive increase in population and information technology, humans are confronted with new situations that instinct nor culture can prepare us for. The use of electronic media has exposed some of humanity to vast informational resources denied to other segments of the population.

The question increasingly becomes how will we use this new technology? To what end? Will we use it to further selfish personal goals and deplete the planet's resources, or will we utilize it to uplift and unite humanity?

Lilly, on the other hand, focuses more on overcoming internal barriers to realization, in the assumption that this will eventually lead to an ultimate unification of purposes with some posited vast universal intellect. While Leary provided the vision, Lilly attempted to find the means of implementation.

Lilly avoided many of the excesses that Leary succumbed to, yet, in his own conservative way, Lilly was even more radical than Leary. Whilst Leary advocated the use of technology to effect evolution, Lilly actually adopted the computer model to describe human consciousness to help remove the temptation of self-indulgence. Like Descartes, Lilly began by doubting everything but consciousness. But he goes beyond Descartes with his description of consciousness as programs to be written and manipulated.

Whether or not the various levels of consciousness posited by both scientists actually exist is still a subject for further exploration and debate. Subjective Reality builds on the work of these two, but goes beyond, to posit a unitive level of being beyond appearances of externals.

While both of these authors seek to remove cosmic consciousness from the realm of religion and securely transplant it into the fertile ground of science, both stress a heightened moral awareness with the achievement of these states. And although neither could be classified as personally religious, both ultimately appeal to a greater intelligence which grants order to the universe.

I believe that Lilly came closer than Leary, in his anticipation of the Star Maker. This vision of a vast, eternal creator behind all conscious experience as the True Self is more in line with Subjective Reality. But both were trained scientists, meaning that they had been thoroughly programmed with an empirical, objectivist worldview. Lilly exceeded his programming through his extensive experimentation with his own consciousness, whilst Leary had subjective intuitions, but, in my opinion, never fully transcended his own personality and cultural programming

In general, I have found that many researchers have flirted with the edges of Subjective Reality, but few have dared to cross into that terra incognita. Few academic researchers dare to go there, as it is a sure way to secure professional ostracizing. To my knowledge, scientists, psychologists and philosophers alike shy away from these topics because they reveal a logical conundrum at the heart of our accepted cosmology: the only tool we have to investigate the nature of reality – whether it is internal or external – is our own subjective consciousness. This problem undercuts every claim of science to True Objectivity. Few living in the palace want to mention that the Emperor is wearing no clothes.

But if the research of these scientists is on the right path (along with

Advaita Hinduism, Quantum Physics, and some forms of Buddhism and Gnosticism), then it is incumbent upon each of us to learn about and explore these inner realms of consciousness, for in learning about ourselves, we learn about the wellsprings of our experienced reality.

CHAPTER 6
AVATARS

Have you ever stopped to truly consider what a bizarre and mercurial world we live in? We take astonishing things as daily givens, without recognizing how we as a species have come so far so fast. We have learned to manipulate and mutate nature, but have yet to truly understand and fulfill our own inner nature.

When I was a kid, I used to make "computers" out of cardboard boxes and bicycle reflectors raided from my red Schwinn Bantam two-wheeler. Now I am chained to the real thing, first for eight hours a day at work and now on my couch.

When I was a kid watching Star Trek with my dad, I had no idea that computers would be so commonplace, nor did I foresee the whole total pervasiveness of media and technology in our culture in my own adulthood.

We in America are an experiment in lifestyles of a highly specialized order. Our psychic and material ambition and skill are evident in the individualism of our homes and lifestyles. We are more plugged in than any previous generation, and we are proud of it. The internet has added a completely new dimension of social contact than had ever existed before. Internet social networking and the creation of the blog allow an individual unprecedented access to thousands, if not potentially millions, of others around the world. We are extending ourselves into the astral realm of cyberspace and connecting through our avatars, not our bodies.

Yet, I posit that our physical bodies are already our avatars, which our consciousness has downloaded into, but we forgot that a long time ago.

Or maybe we didn't forget, hence the wild popularity of movies like the Matrix and Avatar, as well as computer and video games. All of these media show us a multidimensional reality, mediated through electronics – the ultimate symbol of man's desire for dominion over nature.

We have became accustomed to identifying with our physical bodies and emotions, not with any other part of our being, which blinds us from recognizing the origin of our being. It is this disconnect from the cosmic that allows us to lead small petty lives, hiding the grandeur of our true potential, most especially from ourselves. It is easy to say we are hypnotized by the magic of the media we are awash in, but that would only be superficially true.

The real truth is that if we were to acknowledge our greatness, we would be overwhelmed and the small, petty self swept away. So we may have some dim idea of the other reality, but we fail to grasp a hold of it out of a twisted sense of self-preservation. So we remain blind and ignorant of our true nature, focusing instead on manipulating some piece of nature into technology we can use.

We mimic our own nature in the creation of our electronic selves. These electronic selves are often highly crafted and edited, as we only show the world those sides of us that we want them to see. Without the feedback system of voice and actual body language cues, 80% of complete communication is lost to electronic forms of communication and "entertainment."

Unfortunately, to accept one reality is to reject the other. So those who are alive to the other reality have a choice to make. Which reality will you live and extend yourself into?

The paralyzing realization is that to choose one reality is to turn your back on the other. Of those who are aware enough to see the choice, most are stuck, caught on the horns of the dilemma – which reality is really real? If I put all my chips on one side, I might lose it all. But if I win, I win big.

CHAPTER 7
RADICAL IDEALISM

[Author's Note: This essay was originally written while I was in graduate school, so it is a bit technical. It does a really good job explaining how Subjective Reality (or as I called it here, Radical Idealism) works, as I see it. It also gives an excellent account for Personal Identity inside Monism. I have updated and expanded some parts, both for clarity and because my understanding has grown in the decade since this was composed.]

"As above, so below, but like unto another manner."
- Alchemical Maxim

Introduction

In Philosophy, a "Universal" is the term often used to describe a property that can be applied universally, such as "hot," or "round" or "shiny." Universals are qualities that an individual might have, such as "a Fluffy Orange Cat." "Fluffy" and "Orange" are both

Universals. But "Cat" would be an individual, also called a Particular, because it is a particular instance of catness that is referred to here. But what is the relationship of universals to individuals? How is it that something unique and individual can also contain something shared?

Philosophers have masticated the metaphysical question of how qualities adhere to particulars for over two thousand years. Now it's my turn. I begin by rejecting the whole premise as false.

Those who speculate the existence of universals, and how those universals relate to particulars, engage in an active dualism, somehow pitting the collective against the individual, heaven against earth, subject against object.

I suggest that perhaps the true state of affairs is otherwise. I propose to argue for Radical Idealism – the existence of a single substance, often called "mind," which resolves the duality and can account for both particulars and universals.

If you remove the inherent dichotomies in everyone from Plato to Quine, you end up with what?... Unity? But how can this unity exist when the existence of any single individual, much less the unending multitudes of individuals and particulars we daily perceive, refutes the existence of unity? In fact, it is my assertion the Platonic Dualism, much like Cartesian Dualism, is a misunderstanding – a confusion of levels of reality for separate realities.

By the way, based on their own writings, I do not believe that either Plato or Descartes suffered from this delusion. It is only those who came after, whose limited understanding and vision prevented them from truly grasping the full import of these two seminal philosophers, that misconstrued the original meaning.

For as long as humanity has existed, mystics of all stripes have denied the subject/object division, even though it seems counter-intuitive to many. Usually, this unitary cosmology was ensconced within a religious context that precluded the majority of humanity. But as science has continued its own path of evolution, current empirical science in the guise of quantum mechanics offers us a cosmology of a unitary nature – or a "Holotropic Universe[1]," as mind researcher Stanislav Grof coins it. To me, this smells suspiciously of that ancient mystic recognition: that the whole is contained within the part.

Having affirmed the essential unity of reality, the next question is: what is that one substance? The traditional answer is God. Other names have been The Unmoved Mover (not Aristotle's), Brahma, Tao, the Ain… A more recent name is *Holomovement* (D. Bohm in Grof, p.9).

But what is this unity of which we are supposedly a part? Is there only matter, with mind being some subtle form of matter? Or is there only mind, which solidifies into matter? If the table and I are essentially one, what is it that we have in common that makes us a unity, despite the appearance of separateness? Matter? Perceptions?

Mystics and quantum scientists have offered various views, a few of which we shall explore. But, ultimately, this may be unanswerable at our present state of development. For the sake of argument, I shall argue that the only substance in existence is mind or consciousness, but I could have chosen matter equally effectively.

"God and microbe are the same system, the only difference is in the number of centers." (G.I. Gurdjeiff, p.209)

Octaves of Reality

So, how am I, my coffee table and God all one unity? Medieval Jewish mysticism (known as *Qabbalah*) holds that there are "worlds within worlds" – in other words, interpenetrating layers of reality, something like holographic nesting dolls.

For the purpose of this enquiry, I shall posit only the four traditional layers of existence, although greater minds than mine have hypothesized more ambitious and far-reaching distinctions and

---

[1] Grof defines the term 'Holotropic' as a "radically expanded model of the human psyche" which includes the study of non-ordinary states of consciousness and quantum mechanics. (Grof, p.20)

conclusions. And it should be noted that this is my own understanding, and not an exposition of Qabbalistic theory, although it is extrapolated from the traditional Qabbalistic Four Worlds. I have changed the traditional Hebrew names for more explicative terms.

These octaves of existence (or experience) are a synthesis of ancient and modern theories, which more or less conform to the accepted traditional models.

The Physical Octave - External Reality

Berkeley argued brilliantly that to exist is to perceive or to be perceived (*Principles,* I,3; p.66). According to this line of reasoning, being is relative – contingent upon the existence of other perceivers. Ideas cannot exist without someone perceiving them. Physical objects are complexes of perception and ideas. Objects have constancy, in Berkeley's idealism, because they are either actively or potentially perceived. That is, the table exists because I or someone else might see it. But in the absence of me (or anyone else) having seen it, the table continues to exist outside my (or anyone else's) range of perception because some mind is still perceiving it (God).

At this point, I part company with Brother Berkeley, as he still admits of an objective reality, which can only be known subjectively, through our senses. To be perceived, in Berkeley's account, is to *be* an idea within a mind. His view, then, posits the existence of at least two substances: mind and ideas. A radical theory of unity denies that more than one substance exists. It denies any split between inner and outer, subject and object.

Yet, how do I account for this seemingly counter-intuitive claim? I have an experience of what appears to be objective reality. My dirty laundry seems to have continued existence, independent of my attention or inattention. How can I assert an absolute unity of existence, when the laundry pile continues to grow, despite my will that it shrink. If I am all there is, then it might seem that my will should prevail.

But this question suffered from the same misunderstanding. I go into more detail with in the next section, the problem of "Level Confusion." Those who ask this type of question are mistaking the desires of their physical level being for being the will of the Whole. Obviously, it is not, otherwise, I would get everything I want, when I want it and the way I want it.

We have become accustomed to thinking of ourselves as the little self/False Self/Ego, but this is but the tip of the iceberg of our being. Current psychological theories hold that 85 – 95% of our mind is below the level of consciousness. That part of us that asserts itself as "Me" is actually an imposter – a mere fraction of our consciousness, masquerading as the whole.

But there does seem to be something guiding the opportunities and synchronicities of my life, as evidenced by re-occurring life patterns and leitmotifs that keep coming back around, time and again. When I look back across the span of my life, I can see the trajectory of the story arc, as well as the eraser dust of the Cosmic Editor. It is our vast unconscious that actually determines our choices and reactions, much more than our conscious ego selves. When we align the unconscious with the Cosmic Editor... *that* is when the magic starts to happen! But I'm getting ahead of myself.

The physical level is the lowest octave (or outermost circle) of manifestation, being constructed of the densest forms of cosmic substance, or Universal Mind. By density, what is referred to here is like unto a wave frequency (or more poetically, a cosmic musical note), as the physically manifesting multiverse is held to be the lowest rate of mental activity (or vibration). The term density, therefore, is not a strictly defining attribute, but rather is an attempt at describing inertial movements of mind at the lowest (and slowest) octave of consciousness.

Following the wave model, it is possible for many different levels to co-exist and interpenetrate simultaneously. These interpenetrating mind-waves (for lack of a better word) are in constant contact with one another, their interactions generating that level of awareness, which we usually label as physical existence. The physical level is only the lowest that we are consciously aware of – for all we know, there may be even lower scales of existence occupying the same time-space continuum with us that are below our ability to register, even with advanced technological aids.

This level of being also includes the concrete mind, as well as all varieties of thought pertaining to physical existence. Just as physics had to redefine itself in the light of its discoveries, so is every field of human inquiry being redefined to accommodate the implications of relativity and uncertainty.

"The exploration of the microworld soon revealed that the universe of everyday life, which appears to us to be composed of solid, discrete objects is actually a complex web of unified events and relationships. Within this new context, consciousness does not just passively reflect the objective material world; it plays an active role in creating reality." (Grof, p. 6) Thus, matter is dependent on mind for its form.

But I go even further and say that only mind exists. Therefore, matter gets both its form *and* its existence from mind (or consciousness), just as music is both sound and vibration. So, if both the form and the being are of the same substance (mind), then it seems reasonable to say that mind and matter are equivalently of the same substance, thus denying substance dualism from the likes of Descartes. The faster and more complex the mind-waves, the higher the level of consciousness.

The Psychological Octave – Inner Reality

Just as physical manifestation is part of the cosmic continuum, so also is the Psychological Octave part and parcel of the whole, and can be understood as existing closest to the Physical. This is the level where the mind-waves are complex and of sufficient momentum to produce self-awareness, such as personal, subjective experiences (read: humans).

But there is also a universal aspect of this level of existence. A good example of the sharing of inner reality is found in the works of C. G. Jung's theories of the Collective Unconscious and Archetypes. Jung hypothesized that all humanity shares not only a subliminal co-awareness (which accounts for phenomena such as synchronicity and ESP, amongst others), but also a shared lexicon of symbols called archetypes. Some might even go so far as to claim that Jung's archetypes are the psychological octave's equivalent of universals. But such speculation is not within the limited scope of this essay.

In the psychological octave, active imagination and emotion, as well as beliefs, contribute to shape the shared perceptions of "reality." The vibratory rate is just beyond the pale of physical perception, being experienced subjectively. This realm also traditionally contains the lower abstract mind.

This is the level that the Law of Attraction and karma operate on. Manifestations in the physical octave are precipitated by the frequencies chosen at the psychological level, either through cause and effect (Karma) or through sympathetic attraction (Law of Attraction/Reality Creation). The Psychological Octave is the link between the Physical and Spiritual. All communication between the Physical and Cosmic octaves must be mediated through the Psychological Realm.

The Spiritual Octave – Cosmic Reality

The spiritual level relates to the higher abstract mind and metahuman consciousness in which humanity participates, such as planetary, solar and galactic consciousness). It is in this nexus of consciousness from which true prophets, mystics and founders of religions arise, as well as from what level the miraculous is accomplished.

Often, this level of being is mistaken for a separate, "higher" level than the physical and psychological. But the truth, in my understanding, is that all levels are interpenetrating, all simultaneously present in all times and spaces, whether the limited consciousness of one level is alive to that possibility or not. This "Level Confusion Error" is very widespread, found in adherents of most religions and spiritual practices.

Heaven is believed to be "out there somewhere," and it's my job to figure out how to get there, either through a particular morality or religious rites or some such mechanism believed to be pleasing to the Deity (or Deities) inhabiting this exclusive Heaven. This view holds that if I am just good/holy/enlightened enough, I can join the club – I can move from *here* to over *there*. This is a materialist construal of non-physical space.

Even those who may manage to raise their own vibratory rate sufficiently to contact the spiritual level can falter in the interpretation of their own experiences. But usually, it is those who come after and read about someone else's direct experience that fail to understand. If you look closely at the language used by the likes of Plato, Jesus and Descartes, you can see a thread of radical idealism weaving throughout.

Like the other octaves of being, the cosmic reality intermingles and influences all other levels of being. It stands between the human range of experience and the Absolute. It's vibratory rate is only felt subjectively by those blessed few, but all lower levels are heavily impacted by the swift, highly complex movements of these dynamos of mind on unconscious and mass levels.

The Metaprogrammic[2] Octave – Ultimate Reality

This octave of being is both the deepest and the most ineffable. It has been variably called: the Tao, the Ain (Negative Veils of Existence) or the Holy Spirit. It is the immediate awareness and presence of infinity, the Ultimate Experiencer, Brahma. The metaprogrammic level of reality is beyond the direct experience of human senses, yet all of existence is contingent upon the existence and consciousness of this center of all being. It has been likened to the silence that underlies the celestial music that we call creation.

I have attempted to describe a theoretical continuum of being and consciousness that permeates and connects the whole universe. The positing of the four interactive layers of being accounts for the

---

[2] This term comes from the works of neurophysicist John Lilly. It refers to the capacity to observe and simultaneously control multiple – in this case, infinite – programs. I choose this term for lack of a better one, as many common terms carry unintended religious or emotional charges.

existence of universals and particulars, as all mind-waves interpenetrate and cooperate.

The intermixing of all these layers of reality into a rich, meaningful, cohesive whole suggests that what we perceive may not always be an accurate reflection of "true" reality. In this paradigm, "reality" is not some fixed external object. For example, the table is not other than me – it is a part of me and I am a part of the table. Both the table's existence and my own are contingent on the existence of everything else – just as everything else that exists is contingent on the existence of both me and the table.

Thus, empirical science no longer holds any stronger claim than any other system of belief. While we might find science helpful in manipulating the Physical Realm, we should not fall into the error of assuming that the discoveries of science are revelations of a "True" Reality. To make that assumption turns the explorations of science into religion.

"We ultimately come to the realization that all perceptions and knowledge – including scientific work – are not objective reconstructions of reality; instead, they are creative activities comparable to artistic expressions. We cannot measure true reality; in fact, the very essence of reality is its immeasurablity." (Grof, p.10)

Particulars

In a dualistic paradigm one must account for individual identity as distinct from universals. But Radical Idealism as described here, does not equate individuality with bundles of attributes. Attributes and properties are accidental to the individuality, which is grounded in essence.

A round, wooden table and a rectangular glass table are both tables, but the physical properties of each are contingent on a single instantiation of the whole cosmos. Attributes and properties confirm individuality, but they don't by any means create it. Each and every part is necessary to the existence of the whole.

This Radical Idealist position shares some features of the nominalist position of Substratum Theory, in which individuals with shared attributes are accounted for by the positing of a substrata underlying the existence of each individual. In Absolute or Radical Idealism, the Whole (interpenetrating realities and all) functions as the substratum of the separate identities of identical objects. Just as in music, every note, every nuance is necessary to the complete whole song. It is how each of the notes' vibrations balance and reflect each other which creates the mood and tune of the music.

The whiteness of a piece of chalk, for instance, is white by virtue of the fact that its mind-waves-stuff vibrates at the level of awareness that our human awareness registers as "whiteness" or "chalkiness." The seeming attributes of the chalk are not intrinsic to its being, but are more likely artifacts of our perception. The true being of the chalk is not what it appears to be to limited human senses, just as the true being of humans are not limited merely to our visible physical bodies.

Just as human minds contain thoughts and ideas mostly hidden from other human minds, so does the chalk contain an awareness of self that we are not able to access subjectively. It is this awareness of "chalkiness" which the chalk contains that humans interpret as white, cylindrical, etc. What are perceived as attributes are the distinct vibratory rates given off by specific complexes of frequencies of mind-waves. The uniqueness of the piece of chalk is found in its awareness (as low and rudimentary as that may seem to us).

Awareness is created at the intersection of mind-waves. The faster and more complex the wave pattern becomes, the higher the level of self-awareness. Yet, all these many levels of mind vibrations are all just aspects of a single Whole, which is always in contact (directly or subliminally) with All-That-Is.

As individuality is contained within (and is not the effect of external reality), there is no need for any elaborate theory to account for separate particulars. All seemingly separate particulars are grounded in the existence of everything else, in an interconnecting web of being. The question of identity is one of ontology, for to understand All As Mind, immediately, the question arises, *"Who's mind?"* The easy answer, of course, is God/The Universe/All-That-Is/Insert-Your-Own-Name.

Universals – The Holotropic Universe

As we saw before, universals exist as a shared consciousness, coined by psychoanalyst C.G. Jung as the "Collective Unconscious," peopled by "Archetypes." Thus, Qualities (Properties) and Kinds are subliminally shared ideas, much like Jung's archetypes are subliminally shared ideas. As all the layers of reality are intermixed, every aspect of the whole contains the pattern of everything within it.

Physicist David Bohm hypothesizes that the reality which we perceive is only a small fraction of the whole of reality. Bohm calls what small amount our senses reveal the "Explicate" order of reality. The larger remaining unperceived reality he calls the "Implicate" order. The Implicate order is the matrix from which the explicate order arises – much as a hologram emerges from the combination of holographic film and coherent light. And, like a hologram, the grand design is imprinted throughout the being of the film, so any portion of it presents a picture of the whole.

Thus, the Implicate order of reality is not directly perceivable, just like the picture of a hologram is not apparent by merely looking at the film, without the laser playing apparatus. Ultimately, the vastness and richness of the Implicate reality confounds our ability to describe the experience of infinity (Grof, p. 9 – 10)

As all existence is but the interactions of individualized aspects of a greater, organic whole, relations are of utmost importance. It is each consciousness' relationship to its neighbors and to the whole, which combines with consciousness to cement the separate identity that originated in the whole.

To return to the music metaphor, it is the relationship of the notes to each other in their relative place that creates the melody. For consciousness on the human level, it is the positing of location within space/time which brings separate entities into relationship in the Explicate order.

Objections and Responses

1) *The first obvious objection to Radical Idealism is the lack of empirical or intuitive evidence to support it. If we are all connected to some Cosmic Whole, why don't I feel it? Why hasn't science proven it?*

Although I believe I answered this charge in the body of the paper, my first response is to point to the works of those scientists already noted, who hold to this same (or a very similar) view of Radical Idealism. They come from several different disciplines, ranging from Quantum Physics (David Bohm), to Neurophysiology (John Lilly) to Psychology (Stanislav Grof). The fact that these researchers all reached the same conclusion through the pursuit of their own respective fields seems rather compelling. Each of them is well respected and often cited in their fields and out.

My second response is that the subliminal subject/object bonding of the nature of the multiplicity of interlaced realities prevents us from ever hoping to obtain any "purely objective" evidence of anything at all. The objection is just as non-verifiable as the assertion.

As for the charge of being counter-intuitive, I reply by asking if this is really so? After all, every world religion teaches Radical Idealism in some form or another. Any good mystic worth his salt would tell you the same thing. And so would that purple-haired pierced and tattooed punk raver with the drums hanging out on Campus Corner.

2) Another possible objection to this position is that it implies a religious context, as the Cosmic Holographic Whole looks a lot like a deist God.

Nonsense and Poppycock! I retort!

Obviously, both Grof and Bohm don't think it is contingent on religion. Nor do Lilly or Leary. Now, if you have a taste for some Religion Sauce on your personal reality, feel free to pile it on. C.G. Jung and Journalist Gary Zukav both use religious metaphors to share certain thoughts and insights. Countless mystics have discovered deeper levels of being through prayer and meditation, such as Martin Buber and Yogananda. And, as for equating the whole with God, I say, if the shoe fits...

But I deny a deist God, in the sense that the abolition of the subject/object distinction makes God much more interactive. A Deist God implies a deity that created the cosmos and then took a hike. In Radical Idealism, God is right where you are sitting now (to borrow a phrase from Robert Anton Wilson).

3)   *If everything exists in essential unity, how can anything maintain an individual identity? If I am only a molecule in God's toenail, how come I still experience myself in the singular? And, of course, what about Free Will?*

I repeat my refrain: the fusion of subject and object prevents the dissolution of identity in the whole. Each aspect is a part of the whole and is integral to the composition of the whole. The whole cannot exist without every one of its parts. Thus, consciousness (as the only existing substance) is conserved, though it's precepts, maxims and archetypes can and will change form.

As far as the question of Free Will goes, I assert that Radical Idealism is an affirmation of Free Will. It is only by Free Will that we continually partake in and shape the reality we perceive through our beliefs and desires. It could not come to pass that an individual wills something that is perceived to be at odds with the will of the whole. Again, the subject/object fusion chimes in here. If there is no difference between subject and object, there can be no conflict between subject and object.

Therefore, any perception of an individual will in conflict with the collective will must be a misperception – like an optical illusion that resolves once you change your point of reference. Could we perceive the Implicate order of reality, I am sure many such paradoxes would be solved.

4)   *Finally, if everything is mind and consciousness, what are thoughts? Isn't that another substance?*

No. It is not necessary to posit a separate substance to account for thoughts, as thoughts are one of the generally recognized contents of consciousness.

Thoughts are also consciousness, but of a very different order. Thoughts and concepts as we experience them, have their own evolutions, using human minds as the medium of their growth – through sharing a thought, it is increased in strength and complexity. Daniel Dennett offers a nightmarish view of a parasitic evolution of concepts in his discussion of infestations of memes (units of cultural transmission) (Dennett, p. 203- 207).

There are limitless universes and infinite entities within us, and we within them, which we have little to no conscious knowledge of. The depths and heights of our being spin off into infinities large and small, but throughout our being, we have the capacity to recognize ourselves, if we stop to acknowledge it.

But deep within, we *know* in the core of our being, even if we do not know on a conscious level. All the evidence you need can be gathered by looking at any great work of art. What makes any art great is that it solicits a recognition of sameness deep within.

For example, Michelangelo's "Pieta" is great, not only because it is well-executed, but also because it evokes a common human emotional response. The works of Shakespeare are considered great because the Bard was able to pin down in iambic pentameter the heights and depths of the human spirit, and we all recognize ourselves in his keen insights. It is this common recognition that is the echo of our actual state of being.

Conclusion

This essay has explored my conception of Radical Idealism. By dissolving the subject/object distinction, I have posited the existence of one substance: Mind. Within this one substance of infinite densities and varieties there exists multiple interpenetrating orders of being, roughly analogous to interpenetrating wave patterns. I described four possible orders of being, and how their interaction creates Implicate and Explicate orders of reality.

A single substance theory eliminates the need for those messy nominalist accounts of identity and attributes. According to Ockham's Razor, the simplest theory is most likely to be right.

Well, you can't get any simpler than One.

CHAPTER 8
THE MEANING-DRIVEN LIFE

It is all about You – but not the little ego you. Rather, life is all about connecting with the bigger You – your Inner Self. This is the journey of all spiritual quests and the Ultimate Goal of all seeking: to find and unite with the larger part of your Self that has always been one with the Universe – the part of yourself unlimited by circumstances and fears.

The Inner Self is the source of all meaning and true purpose in life. Find it, and you know who you are and why you are here. Without it, you are alone and helpless in a hostile world.

The default world can give you purpose. It can give you enough mindless busywork and daily mandatory routines to spend a whole life without a free moment. But the default world cannot give you meaning. For meaning is created subjectively, inside each of us.

We all have our own unique, individual perceptions and expressions. And when we withhold those unique perceptions and expressions in conformity to the purposes of the world, we deny both the Universe and our brother and sister humans the divine expression we were created to embody.

There must be the possibility of transcendence for life to make sense to me. Without a concept of consciousness surpassing the limitations and default settings of biology, creation seems pointless and random. In other words, without meaning. If all I have to live for is the perpetuation of biological functions in myself and others, and all the simian politics that goes with our primate heritage, then I don't want to play.

I have always felt that there was a lot more to me than is manifest here in this little fuzzy animal body, and more beauty and knowingness in me, than contained within the 3.5 pounds of grey jelly in my skull. The affairs of personal, professional and national politics and finances are not sufficient to give meaning to life. For me, happiness is impossible without meaning.

Years ago, when divorcing from my first husband, I made a conscious decision that any time there was a choice to be made that, meaning would be my primary criteria. Any time I had to choose between two or more options, I resolved to always choose the option which had the most resonance for me personally. I have never regretted that decision, although it has taken me down some very strange paths!

The conscious transcending of biology (aka Waking Up, Switching Off the Autopilot, Enlightenment, Increasing Awareness, Evolving, etc) seems to me the most important thing we can devote our lives to. While tending to family and career is often commendable, it pales in comparison to the importance of waking up.

But this awakening is tremendously difficult in our present day consumer culture, because the monkey mind (lower brain functions) are so easily distracted and entranced, and then autopilot takes over the whole mechanism, instead of being used as a vital part of a much larger and more complex system. Autopilot (habits, and entranced repetitive behaviors) is useful in its place, but when one acts from habits and entranced patterns picked up randomly and without consideration or intention, then one is at the mercy of external and circumstantial forces with no way to assert or retain conscious direction.

These habits and entranced behavior patterns are the product of the older, more "reptilian" parts of the brain. Our sense of self-consciousness is believed by researchers to be housed in the neo-cortex, the most evolutionarily recent development of our brains. These older structures in the brain (sometimes called the "Lizard Brain") can exert considerable influence on our personal behavior and unfolding, especially if certain structures and capacities in the brain are not fully developed.

Hence, we often find ourselves "highjacked" by emotions or thoughts based on lower brain functions, such as low self-esteem, fear, perceived self-preservation or bodily desires, such as lust, hunger and obsession, which prevent us from achieving the clarity necessary for accessing our higher brain functions.

There are some researchers and commentators on the human condition who believe we have gone astray from our evolutionary path and are now going up a possible dead end. Others believe we are just 'going through a difficult phase' in our evolutionary development, that we will soon outgrow.

Either way, it seems clear to me that we must assert conscious intention to get us out of the current political, cultural and environmental messes we have collectively created through the unthinking following of the promptings of our lower selves.

While living in the most privileged society on the planet, many of us feel unfulfilled, frustrated and trapped in lives we did not want to have, but ended up with either by default or by mistake. We sometimes feel cheated out of an unknown life we somehow 'should' have had – that we are not allowed to express our true selves due to the limits placed on us by others or by our own fears.

Many spiritual teachers and traditions tell us that it is not our failures that we fear, rather, it is our greatness which we are frightened to let show. But this need not be our fate. We can choose to allow our Deeper Self to inject meaning and purpose into our existence. But it takes time and patience to undo a lifetime of unconscious habits and decisions.

Like with developing our physical muscles, we can develop the capacities and strengths of our conscious minds to resist the tendency to live on autopilot, instead of using it judiciously to achieve our intentions and goals.

As G.I. Gurdjieff noted, a certain amount of psychic momentum is required in order to break the entrancement of the lower brain structures. This momentum is built through the use of positive, intentional habits (in the philosophical field of Virtue Ethics, these are called virtuous habits) because human will power is insufficient when undeveloped. Will power is a limited resource that requires frequent re-charging (somewhat like my cell phone!). Good habits can often carry us even when our will power is weak. But the question then arises: what kinds of habits are necessary to transcendence?

In order for consciousness to transcend biology, we must attain the habits of expanded consciousness: regular meditation and contemplation (two different things), intentional creative pursuits and the regular exposure to what Gurjieff called "conscious material," that is, literature and art created consciously in a space of intentionally increased awareness.

So what is this consciousness and what is it's goal?

Consciousness is that within you that knows and knows that it knows. It is that continuity of awareness that remains untouched through all of the many phases, changes and circumstances of our lives.

If we are truly embodied spiritual creatures (as I believe we are), then why did we come here? Surely it was not merely to consume, reproduce and die. The ecology of nature would argue against such a cosmic waste of potential. If we are truly aspects of divinity, then in order for our existence to have meaning, we must have come here to this plane of existence in order to fulfill a divine mission.

So, as spirits embodied, it seems our mission is to recognize our position and to attain the habit of identifying with the eternal aspects of ourselves, rather than limiting our awareness to the ephemeral aspects associated with biological survival and reproduction.

But this is difficult to accomplish, because our minds are unaccustomed to holding fixed thoughts and perceptions for very long. The ephemeral conditioning of biology entrances us with an ever-changing set of variables we must navigate. I call this being "Velcro-ed™."

It is very easy to forget about the option of seeing life from a larger (divine) context. It is easy to get sucked into two-dimensional thinking of established neural patterns (i.e. paths of least resistance) rather than to look for the broadest perspective you can handle. It is much easier to be self-protective, rather than inclusive.

Our brains are biologically conditioned to run on autopilot (i.e. the path of least resistance), as well as genetically pre-disposed towards certain habits and configurations. But just because our autopilot has certain default settings that we may not like, that does not mean we are doomed forever by biological determinism – unless we refuse to claim the power of our consciousness to rise above and re-set the defaults on our autopilot to more agreeable settings.

Again, this is not a quick or easy task, but it appears to be necessary for humanity to move forward as a species, as well as for individuals to move forwards in their own personal journeys.

Without transcending our biological drives, humanity is locked into a zero-sum game of dwindling resources and expanding populations. Only the expansion of consciousness can get us out of inevitable conflict and suffering. Expanded horizons and vision can help us to navigate the turmoil of embodiment, avoiding foreseeable crashes and enabling unimpeded progress. Unleashed divine creativity imagines new solutions and inspired combinations to our problems. Third and even fourth dimensional thinking lifts us up out of duality and gives us wider understanding – imparts the vision to encompass both divinity and biology simultaneously.

We are conditioned by biology from the get-go – our sex, the efficiency and completeness of our organs and bodily systems all impact the quality and content of our lived experience. If we are born into a severely malfunctioning or handicapped body, our existence will primarily focus on surviving that handicap or dysfunction. If we become injured, diseased or aged, our lives often become focused on dealing with the consequences of these conditions.

But despite the narrowing of focus to the biological, we still have Free Will in how to understand our conditioned life – we can choose to see our physical conditions as a blessing or a curse. I am reminded of the grace and spirituality with which actor Christopher Reeve embodied after his severe spinal cord injury, which paralyzed him from the chest down and eventually ended his life after several years of brave struggle. He truly was a super-man, although he could no longer even walk or breathe unassisted, much less fly.

We get to decide whether life is something we endure or something we enjoy. Our consciousness orients our emotional and intellectual and spiritual responses to the limitations imposed by embodiment.

All religion points away from embodiment to identification with spirit (consciousness). Many religions tend towards asceticism – the rejection and chastising of the body, in the belief that mortification of the flesh automatically leads to identification with consciousness – but this is not necessarily true.

Asceticism can succeed if the aspirant can let go of his identification with the body and shift his sense of self to include his own Inner Self. But all too often, instead what is engendered is a hatred and rejection of the biological element of our being, setting up the conditions vibrationally for obsession, future disease and accidents.

Culture further deepens our disdain of the biological in numerous ways: by holding up unachievable images of beauty and physical configurations; by over-sexualizing advertising; through the healthcare and insurance industry's stranglehold on mainstream conceptions of health and illness... These are just a few of the ways our culture forces us to identify with our bodies, but then sets up barriers to our acceptance of our bodily beingness.

We fear our bodies' power to shape our experiences because we do not understand what we are existentially and how our consciousness relates to our bodies. On one hand, we are taught by culture that we ARE our bodies and this one is all we get. But our predominant religions tell us we are NOT our bodies and must seek salvation. With the decline in religion as a real live spiritual power (not merely a political power) in most postmodern Westerners' lives, we have come to focus on our bodies as much more than a game avatar, rather, we have come to believe that the body is our Self. Nowadays, we are taught that we as a species are limited and conditioned by our bodies.

Yet how we interpret and express inside those conditions is entirely up to us. Biology may "throw" us into unchosen circumstances, but how we orient and respond is an expression of our consciousness. We may be born into a failing and feeble body, such as physicist Stephen Hawking was, but, like Hawking, we can choose to transcend the conditions imposed by biology through the exercise of consciousness.

Consciousness is always a choice – never a default.

It's all about what part/image of yourself you identify with. If you believe you ARE a body, then your identity is bound by biology. If you identify with an eternal/divine aspect, you transcend genetic predisposition, disease and accident. Choice of destiny then becomes possible, but as long as we identify with our bodies, we are fated to be limited by them.

It's easy to get caught up in the roller coaster ride of physical embodiment: it's so distracting, so entertaining, so exasperatingly PRESENT.

It is easy to lose your perspective amidst the constant swirling of postmodern life. But it is precisely this constant busy-ness that keeps us from identifying with the larger context of the Deep Self. Depth of self-knowing requires both conscious choice and stillness. The busy distracted monkey mind cannot tune into the higher frequencies of the Expanded Self.

We must still our minds and allow the swirling conceptual dust to settle down in order to establish contact with the Larger Self. But once the mind IS trained to settle down, the Larger Self is readily available to access at any and all times. So, it's a matter of both techniques (such as the meditations and exercises in this book) plus remembering to use your techniques while in the thick of the bio-swirling.

From an existential point of view, we exist in a profound state of ignorance – we know very little about the origins and possible purpose of the universe, of life and of ourselves. We don't know why we are born or what happens after we die. We don't know if this is an intended or random universe.

Religion was created to deal with the psychological pain and isolation of this ignorance. Religion is learned, although the religious/spiritual impulse is innate and seems to be hardwired in. (See: Newberg, *Why God Won't Go Away*) How that spiritual impulse is interpreted is both subjective and cultural. We interpret our own spiritual impulses according to our social conditioning – both inherited and chosen. ("Once a Catholic, always a Catholic/recovering Catholic.")

We become fixated and distracted by the external world because it is loud and explicit. The internal world is subtle and silent. Some fear the silence, for they fear confronting themselves without dilution. They fear discovering inadequacy, hypocrisy or cruelty. So they choose to remain in ignorance, rather than risk learning something about themselves and the universe that they may not like. Instead, they cling to age-old, worn out beliefs in the hopes of getting some real mileage from the old forms before they collapse. It is often much easier emotionally to look outside, rather than inside.

But inside is where all the miracles take place.

CHAPTER 9
THE UNLIMITED SELF

Our True, Deep Self is completely unlimited by all constraints and laws. Our Deep Self has never been squashed or shut down. Our Deep Self has never been stifled or suffocated. Our Deep Self has never been deprived or abandoned or betrayed. Our Deep Self has never known abuse or experienced loss or fear.

We all most deeply yearn to be our Unlimited Deep Selves – that inner greatness that we know lurks below the surface of our everyday ego mask. We all long to be unleashed to claim our own magnificence, to connect with and participate in All That Is, but the conditions of the world do not seem to support these deep longings of the heart. True magnificence is not limited by conditions and circumstances. We forget this at our own peril.

We allow ourselves to be shut down out of fear. We have become so separated from our Deep Selves that the brightness of a free unfettered consciousness is overwhelming. When we come into contact with the Deep Self, at the beginning we have to take it in small doses – we glimpse our own magnificence and look away.

Peekaboo!

But to fully embrace our own greatness can be like holding a live wire in your bare hand while standing in a puddle if your vibratory rate is not sufficiently high to match. If you are not fully prepared, a serious shock is risked!

So we must acclimatize ourselves to the Deep Self with frequent small exposures, building up our capacity and vibratory rate, not only to behold and embrace the Unlimitedness of the Deep Self, but also to remove the Impediments to the natural expression of our own true greatness.

The Ego is not our friend in this endeavor. The small self distracts us with emotionally charged memories, obsessions and imaginings, fascinating the mind with guilt, shame, desire, fear and whatnot. These all serve to keep our focus on the Lower Self and the body, tempting us to identify exclusively with those lower elements and obscuring the vision of the Deep Self and its realm of existence.

We begin to forget about the Deep Self we all once knew so well in early childhood – before we internalized the projections of fear and expectations of others. We forget the Unlimited Self that we truly are when we listen to the incessant chatter of the Ego, and instead identify ourselves with the limited, ephemeral dimension of Self. Therefore, when, in the due course of our personal evolution, we begin to turn back towards the Deep Self, we need to make frequent, intentional visits to the inner stillness of the Deep Self to re-acclimatize.

We can become lost between the two realms when our vision is clouded by attacks of the Ego. We feel the need to defend/justify/prove ourselves when we listen to the Ego's stories of guilt, shame, desire, fear and whatnot. We have been tricked into seeing ourselves as limited by our circumstances and stipulations of the ongoing Storyline, instead of seeing through the Storyline to a vaster realm of existence and meaning.

It is the vision of this vaster, more meaningful dimension of the Deep Self that is our salvation from the wages of guilt, shame, desire, fear and whatnot. The vaster vision is what provides context and meaning to the Storyline. All true religions teach this, but many misconstrue its true implications.

The larger context, the vast vision of the Deep Self is the true bedrock of existence and meaning. Without this broader context, we are spiritually blind and uninspired. Inspiration is linked to vision. Without an expanded vision, you cannot be inspired. If our understanding and identification is confined to only the physical, emotional and political dimensions of being, a crisis of vision is inevitable, as the physical and lower psychic elements cannot provide a meaningful enough context. Despair comes quickly to those who have no higher vision of themselves.

We can also fall into despair when transitioning levels, if we receive the vision of the Deep Self but fail to fully identify with it. If we have sight of the Deep Self but can see no clear path to reach and attain it, we see the Ego's world as meaningless and empty, but no way to break free from it's imprisonment.

We see two worlds then: one world we want and another world we no longer want. One filled with Truth and love, the other filled with illusions, lies and death. We aspire to the brighter reality of our Deep Self, but cannot figure out how to escape the Ego's clutches in the illusory world. Fear, guilt and shame keep us frozen in the past until we choose to recognize that only identification with the Deep Self can resolve the inner rift. The realm of the Deep Self provides the meaning and context the Ego cannot give.

But identification with the Deep Self does not require permanent sequestering away from the lower realms – that is impossible in the body. What is required is to still the mind often and regularly enough to develop new neural responses to the Ego's habituated patterns and ploys for attention. It requires a focusing of intention long enough to outlast the Ego's games – until contact with the Deep Self is secured.

This will over time raise the vibratory level that makes frequent and deeper contact possible. But the motivation for this must come from within. No one else can do it for you or force you to do it against your will, although others can do it along with you, and encourage your persistence.

This motivation can be found in many places, several of them unlikely. It doesn't matter if you are motivated by fear or love at first. What matters is that you are sufficiently motivated to make the effort to contact and identify with the Deep Self. Even dark motivations will be purified as they approach the Light, if the effort is sincere and consistent. Even fear of death can (and often does) serve to bring about identification with the eternal. This is exactly what led to the initial awakening of Ramana Maharshi.

Despair can turn into inspiration if pushed to its logical extreme. Failure comes from half-efforts: distractions, undigested fears and passions – these can keep us in limbo indefinitely if we do not relentlessly follow them fully to their conclusions.

We must be willing to look at our inner fears and desires head-on, and be willing to see the Truth about ourselves. When we fear to look within all of the dark corners, we run the risk of not completing our developmental tasks on this plane of being. The only way out, as they say, is through.

We cannot avoid confronting our deepest fears and most embarrassing failures if we want to progress. For as long as we hang on to judgments of others (such as: mean, scary, fat, trashy, greedy, etc.), we are bound to judge ourselves as well. And if that harsh inner critic should find you wanting, you will limit your own capacity to connect with the Deep Self, in a negative feedback loop. Perhaps you might be familiar with this drill already.

A Random or a Meaningful Universe? You Choose.

A main problem in the acceptance of identification with the Deep Self, rather than the Ego persona, is the implied acceptance and adoption of a teleological universe. Although the vast majority of Americans reportedly believe in a higher power, few seem to have really thought out the implications of what this means, especially as it relates to their worldviews.

We *say* we believe in God, but we do not *behave* as if we do. Instead, we *act* like we believe in technology, in modern medicine, in the limitations of the human body and mind, and conversely, in the ingenuity of man to save us, far more than we behave like believers in an All Mighty God or God's Mercy. We act like we believe in money and profits, in sickness and in death, far more than we act like we believe in eternity and forgiveness. We act like we believe in hatred and fear and war more than we act like we believe in oneness, peace and love.

So even if we adopt and faithfully practice the social customs traditionally associated with belief in an All-Powerful Creator, our day-to-day choices often do not reflect a long-term view from the Deep Self. In fact, they rarely seem to do so. Despite protestations to the contrary, the vast majority of us these days are Scientific Materialists, identifying with the body and its experiences, accepting physical evidence as the ultimate source of Truth, especially in areas of health and medicine.

Theologically, we may call ourselves monotheists, but functionally, we are atheists. That same pronouncement of God's functional death that Nietzsche made over one hundred years ago not only holds true today, but has grown unchecked. Nietzsche's prescience is still to be fully grasped by all but a few. God is dead and we have killed him. We kill him anew every time we seek a technological fix for our spiritual ailments.

Even if we do eschew a Creator, either intellectually, emotionally or functionally, the prospect of the Deep Self remains. It is closest to us and most far. The Deep Self does not demand belief. The Deep Self simply is. And it is readily available for exploration by anyone willing to take the time and focus for self-exploration in earnest silence.

The Deep Self does not require or give empirical proof of its existence. But contact with the Deep Self is obvious and immediate. For those who have touched it, it is more real than the breath you now take.

The vastness of the Deep Self may intimidate at first, but it is the connection to All-That-Is that everyone seeks. Its gift is vision. When we gain the perspective of the Deep Self, our lives and the whole world is put into context.

It is natural and expected for a character in a story to identify with it's own story. But an actor in a film or play always maintains an awareness of her life beyond and transcending the current production she is now playing in. We are like actors who have forgotten everything about our real lives and instead have come to believe we are actually the characters we are portraying.

CHAPTER 10
TIPS FOR ESCAPING THE LIMTED SELF
PART 1: CREATING GOOD HABITS OF MIND

Those who we call "enlightened" are those who have come to identify with the Deep Self, rather than the Limited Self of the personal Storyline. They have recognized their true nature and habituated themselves to the point of view of the Deep Self.

It is tremendously difficult to habituate oneself to identification with the Deep Self, as the personal storyline of the ego-body (Limited Self) is so compelling and immediate. But it all begins with the recognition that identification *can* be *CHOSEN* – it does not have to be biologically based (i.e. tied to the events of the ego-body).

In Plato's Tripartite Soul model, this is equivalent to the permanent balance of Reason over the Emotions and Bodily Instincts. Whenever our emotions or biological drives run away with us, we are not only unbalanced, but we are also unable to see the Deep Self, much less identify with it.

We must first recognize that there is another way and then we must exercise our will in choosing to find and follow the Deep Self. Patience is also required, as our culture does not usually equip us with the tools and skills required for shifting our awareness of identification.

Preparing to Meet the Deep Self

The Deep Self is closer to us than our own heartbeat, but we are distracted and confused by the ever-changing Storyline of the Limited Self (ego-body).

Contacting the Deep Self requires quiet and stillness – two things in short supply in this day and age. Western culture is not set up to be supportive of finding the Deep Self – indeed, it seems as if everything is set up to deter success in finding our true selves. Culture competes with the Deep Self, as does the biologically-based storyline of the Limited Self.

The Storyline of postmodern human life is so compelling and engrossing that it is easy to forget that the Deep Self even exists, and to focus wholly on the biologically-based storyline and its games. We can choose to believe that our existence is all about the bio-emotional roller coaster ride of life, or we can choose to believe that there is a goal of existence beyond serving the needs of biological evolution. We can choose to seek the wider perspective of the Deep Self, above and beyond the storyline of human embodiment.

The Deep Self does not require asceticism to rise above the lure of human embodiment, although asceticism can be helpful at times to help loosen identification with the body. But there is a danger that asceticism can become an obsession, fixated on the body and depriving it. Then, asceticism becomes an end in itself and is no longer useful in achieving the Deep Self. In these cases, such practices become means of furthering one's sleep, as opposed to waking up.

Before full identification with the Deep Self can be achieved, the Will must be strengthened through regular habit and the life must be arranged in such a way that will and energy is not leaked in unhelpful ways. The less attention spent on mundane matters, the more attention is available to find and focus on the Deep Self.

This is not advice to ignore or neglect the duties of your life, but rather, the suggestion of finding ways to streamline routine matters in your life, so you will not need to devote as much time and thought to them. The more daily habits that can be created to free up will and attention resources from survival needs and daily grind stuff, the more resources are available in contacting the Deep Self.

★ *Ultimately, the task of re-connection with the Deep Self is all about Energy – having sufficient energy accumulated to break through all Ego Barriers and Defenses.*

Remove as many potential needless energy-sucks as possible in advance through the inculcation of good habits. Some suggestions on how to create and institute good habits will be given in the next section.

To begin your journey within, give yourself the gift of stillness regularly, where you can sink into the depths of the Self. Allow the sweetness of the Deep Self to envelop you as often and as much as possible.

This simple form of contact with the Deep Self raises the vibratory rate of the biological body, allowing easier access to the Deep Self and acclimatizing you to the higher frequencies of your innermost being.

Don't worry if you do not know what to do or if your attention drifts – this is to be expected, especially at first. Just take time every day to sit quietly and think about your Deep Self, even if you don't really yet have a clear image of what or who that might be. It doesn't matter in the beginning. Simply taking the time to sit and BE with yourself is enough to start building up your spiritual willpower.

Recent studies in Cognitive Psychology suggest that the will is like a muscle and must be built up over time. It also suggests that it is of no use to force yourself, because, like a muscle, when the will's capacity is maxed out, further efforts will not succeed. So be gentle with yourself, and just allow yourself to develop the habit of sitting quietly and looking within.

Devote whatever amount of time works for you to start, and gradually extend the length of time. But above all, do not force yourself, for you will create negative psychological blocks that will prevent you from going deeper later. If you naturally feel inclined to sit for longer, by all means, do so whenever possible, but do not make a chore of it, or you will undermine all your efforts.

Creating Good Habits

In philosophy, Virtue Ethics stresses the importance of having good habits. Excellence, according to Virtue Ethics, is essential to the achievement of a flourishing, happy life (*Eudaemonia* in Greek), and depends on the ownership of good habits. Good habits train our brain – they give us a higher level 'path of least resistance' which is always above reproach, so we are automatically moral people. But good habits also provide maximum efficiency, thereby also improving excellence. Excellence can be understood here as reliable competence.

Good habits are often praised in our culture and in all cultures, but rarely are we taught how to acquire them for ourselves. Good habits can be seen from the point of view of brain conditioning.

It's an old joke that humans were not handed an owner's manual for our human bodies, much less our minds. And for most people, if we had gotten an owner's manual, it would likely be lost, torn up or thrown away by the time we would be mature enough to truly understand its nuances and implications.

And to compound our dilemma, even if we had the instructions, each of us is so unique – an individual expression of the Cosmos coming to know Itself – that those instructions would still likely be insufficient to help us explore and own the specific and individual expression of Oneness that we all are. Therefore, we are left on our own to figure out who and what we are to be.

When we are born to a specific set of parents, in a specific location, we are set upon a baseline trajectory. Unless energy (in the form of conscious intention and action) can be introduced at the right points in the trajectory, the tendency will be to follow the original trajectory to its natural conclusion – biological human life: birth, physical maturation, reproduction, decline and then, death.

Most people do this – they live in the same place, having much the same kind of lives as those around them. Not much effort of intention is required to follow the original trajectory. It is the lower path of bio-emotional least resistance, neurologically-speaking. This is the life of mediocrity – the life of quiet desperation.

Excellence (and Eudaemonia) requires intention – the intention to put your best foot forward. Mediocrity is content with a 'good try' that's 'good enough' to satisfy bio-emotional minimal survival requirements. Excellence asks more of us. Excellence asks us to extend ourselves by choice beyond the minimum required, to test our limits and unleash our creativity.

As human beings, we are each endowed by our creator with a wide array of amazing talents and capacities. Yet , for most of us, the limits of our capacities are rarely tested. Far too often, we settle for 'good enough.' We often do not challenge ourselves to reach for the gold – although we readily admire and praise and may even envy those who do strive to be the best version of themselves that they can envision.

We are often too afraid of failure, unsure of what to do, or worse, ignorant of what we want, to reach for excellence. Multitudes of volumes have been written about overcoming these all too common impediments. Many are fine and useful, as are the many psychological approaches developed and deployed to help.

But the problem is not how to help those already actively seeking professional help for diagnosed issues. The real problem – the greatest waste of potential – is all of us who know we are capable of much more than we are currently giving to the world, but, for whatever reason, we are holding back. We are not fully expressing and exploring who and what we are, often blaming others for our lack of opportunity. But opportunity starts inside our heads!

Excellence, then, starts with the recognition that you can choose how much care and attention you will give to all your tasks. But to have full attention and care given to the present at all times is the attainment of Buddhahood.

So while we recognize that increased attention is necessary for excellence, we also recognize that our consciousness might not be there yet. Therefore, we are still subject to distraction, intimidation and failure. But we can also choose to see these things as lessons to challenge us into excellence, instead of being paralyzed, angry or discouraged. The excellent aren't born that way – they learned and worked on it.

This is where inculcating good habits is crucial, because human attention (or will power) is a limited resource. There is a limit to what we can force ourselves to do. There is a natural "set point" for self-discipline that we tend to adhere to. This "set point" will click on when we are in danger of exceeding our generally established parameters, stopping us from progressing. This is an inner defense mechanism, originally designed to help us maintain homeostasis and avoid system overloads.

Do not despair if your natural "set point" for self-discipline is lower than you would like. These "set points" are changeable, so that, with focused effort, you can increase your capacity for self-discipline. There are ways to strengthen your will power like muscles, so that you also hone your attention focusing capacity.

The long boring hours spent at school taught us how to focus enough on consensus reality to get by, but the school system is not set up to teach excellence. Our school systems are set up to provide foundational functional enculturation, to provide minimally skilled workers for a by-gone manufacturing era, and nothing more. Some are able to thrive in this environment. Many are not and learn to expect boredom and to be content with 'good enough.'

Boredom is impossible when you are trying your best. Boredom is the opposite of intention. Boredom is a signal of lacking intention. If you are often bored, it may indicate a lack of focus on your part – perhaps revealing a deeper lack of clarity of purpose and meaning in life.

Focus and clarity for increased attention can be strengthened through practices, particularly through developing good habits. By having reliable good habits in place, much mental and physical energy, as well as time and resources, can be saved.

This is the thought behind automation and robotics – if the repetitive stuff can be covered automatically, more energy, time and resources are freed up for other, more creative endeavors.

And so it is with us, as well as with manufacturing. The development of good habits is the biological equivalent of the role of robotics in manufacturing. Once you've quit having to search for your keys every day, you've got more time, energy and emotional space for other things.

So how do we start to develop good habits?

A little bit at a time – through baby-steps. Its rare that we can step full-blown into a radically different habit pattern.

That is why most New Year's resolutions and diets fail. You can't just will yourself into a new way of being overnight. The "set points" kick in eventually, and unless sufficient intention is provided to counteract the automatic unconscious process, you will lose interest, get distracted, freak out, or otherwise give up on your resolution to turn a new leaf. And back into your old ways, you will slide...

★ **It takes time to overcome the momentum of the bad habits you are trying to break.** But, as I noted earlier, will power is a limited resource that takes time to recharge once it's depleted. This is called "Ego-Depletion" by Social Cognitive Psychology. This is what accounts for all those cycles of dieting and binging.

★ **The trick is to not overstrain the limits of will power by expecting too much too soon, but rather, build up to your desired new habit, a bit at a time.**

★ **If you make the desired new good habit something convenient, then it will be easier to remember and keep.** For example, if the mailbox key is always returned to the same central location, it will always be both easy to find and easy to return. But if the location is inconvenient, the key is less likely to be returned, rendering the desired new good habit to not be adopted or remembered.

★ So, first of all, **good habits have to go with the flow as much as possible. Use the momentum of already established patterns to work in your favor.**

★ **If you can't remember your desired new habit, it's useless. So remembering your new intention is also important.** When you are working to kick off a new habit, you must introduce extra energy into the system sufficient enough to overcome old patterns of unconscious behavior. Most new good habits fail not because they were not good ideas, but rather, because they were implemented ineffectively. Try to set things up to make it easy to keep your new habit.

In other words, you are using your conscious mind to reset the "set points" in your unconscious mind. But the human mind is not like a thermostat, where you just set it once and walk away.

★ **With the human brain, learning occurs through repetition. We have to repeat things in order to internalize them.**

So, when starting a new habit, we can expect to fall off the wagon. How much we fall off is an indication of what amount of effort will be required to overcome the momentum of your old behavioral patterns.

Don't waste your time or energy blaming yourself or feeling bad about yourself. Just use the experience as vital information and feedback, and adapt your efforts accordingly.

This is where many people become discouraged – when they realize how flabby their minds are and how much effort is required to live a deliberate life. Again, this is where good habits can make all the difference.

★ **Rewarding yourself for small victories is also important strategy for maintaining motivation. Reward yourself often when you do remember your desired new habit, to give positive reinforcement.** Rewards can be anything from a break to a longed-for treat. Just be sure to keep your rewards in line with your ultimate intentions.

Habits are the conscious application of the mind and intention to create a new path of least resistance in the brain more congruent with our goals and desires. Of course, in order to be truly effective, we must be clear about what our goals and desires are – but that's a whole different topic!

CHAPTER 11
TIPS FOR ESCAPING THE LIMITED SELF PART 2:
THE FUNCTIONAL ACTION OF FORGIVENESS

As long as you limit forgiveness, you will find your limits being tested.

Forgiveness is not something you hoard and then measure out sparingly, on an 'as needed' basis. Forgiveness is not a gift you bestow undeservedly to the guilty and incompetent.

Forgiveness is a gift of freedom you give to yourself. When you forgive another's trespasses, you are releasing the bonds of guilt, fear and hatred that have imprisoned *you*.

When you perceive yourself or another as guilty, you are identifying both yourself and that other person with the biological order alone. You are limiting how much of the Deep Self can be manifest.

Guilt is always related to the body: behavior, or thought/speech about behavior. But if the point of perspective is shifted to that of the Deep Self, then all time and space is transcended. The specific behavior of a specific body at a specific time/space coordinate is insignificant to the splendor of diversity that is the Eternal Infinite, in which all possibilities are realized.

In other words, identification with the biological/physical aspect of our being prevents the perception of the quantum universe. When we identify with the Storyline, we forget about the Deep Self.

Sickness can be understood as a kind of statement – a statement about the condition of the small self. Biology is highly suggestive, especially to repeated thoughts and statements. That is one reason why self-talk is so important to monitor. How you talk to yourself in the privacy of your own mind reveals much about your relationship to and true opinion of your self.

We use sickness in many ways: to get sympathy, to enforce a break in activity, to punish ourselves and others, or to achieve a radical transformation. Our culture takes a materialist, bottom-up view of causation: we get sick because we were exposed, our immune system was weakened, something went wrong with our bodies... We hide from life in our sickened bodies.

But when we learn to forgive ourselves and others, we release ourselves from the bondage of a limited understanding of the Self. Forgiveness allows us to step out of the sickness Storyline (even if only momentarily) and to connect with the wholeness of the Deep Self.

But as long as you withhold forgiveness from anyone, you have locked yourself into the biological dimension, where sickness and death are to be dreaded. And as long as you withhold forgiveness, you will be driven by all the fears that attend a limited perception of existence.

Setting up a negative feedback loop, these fears perpetuate hypnotic focus on the biological as the only dimension of your reality. The emotions are whipped up into even greater fear of suffering and loss of the body, making forgiveness even more scarce.

To escape all this, you have to let it go and stop identifying with the Character in the Storyline. *That* **is the functional action of forgiveness.**

It's for *you***, not for them.**

The task of this plane of being is to awaken to the Deep Self, and all occurrences and situations will eventually lead to this goal over the course of human evolution. The problem in any given lifetime is that we do not persistently pursue our questions to their final goal. Instead, we get distracted by the details of the changing Storyline and stray from our deep focus on the Self.

The dimension of the Deep Self is always present, separated from us by only the filmiest of veils. It takes but our persistent intention to access it. Unfortunately, our focus is weak and we are easily distracted and forgetful. The Will must be developed over time, until it garners enough strength to be persistent and sufficiently focused to raise the vibratory rate and break through the unconscious patterns that keep us stuck in the Storyline.

If the intention is clear enough, everything in the Storyline can be used as fuel for the Will. This is done through a combination of consensus actions and the inculcation of good habits – automating as much as possible in order to free up conscious energy for the remembrance and exercise of the Will to access the Deep Self.

The only thing any teacher or guru can teach is their own story – their own journey, what worked for them or those they witnessed. But each and all of have our own unique journey, so the most that any teacher can really do is to encourage students to embrace their own unique extraordinary journey. Our stories are beautifully woven and balanced, if we can "un-Velcro™" ourselves enough to step back and objectively consider it.

Like a colorful moving tapestry, the Storyline of our lives range from the absurd to the sublime, from agony to bliss. It's richness, depths and overtones are fascinating and emotionally engaging – hence the

"Velcro™ Effect," when we find ourselves haplessly stuck on the roller coaster rides of our lives.

Each of us live inside these Storyline bubbles, Velcro™-ed to the wall most of the time.

The trick is to appreciate the uniqueness of your being which is displayed in the moving tapestry of your life's Storyline, but not to become stuck to it.

It is a question of identification – who are you and what part of yourself do you identify with? Are you the product of the Storyline or are you its observer? Are you a victim, part of the Storyline, limited to the circumference of its bubble, or are you the center from which the Storyline bubble emanates? Which would you rather be?

Enlightenment is the realization that you ARE the Deep Self, not the Limited Self. We may know this intellectually, or have had our own intimations or experiences. The goal is to not get Velcro-ed™ back into the Storyline, but to recognize the Truth that only enlightenment exists, for the Storyline is all made up.

If there is such a thing as Eternal Truth, there can be no time or space in which it does not exist. The question is whether we recognize it or not. And it is our identification and beliefs which determine what we are capable of recognizing. We can only recognize those things we are willing to believe in. If we have no conceptual framework for an idea, we cannot understand or embrace it. So all teachers share their own journeys and understandings, hoping to broaden the students' conceptual framework of what is possible.

Each mind is in complete control of its own beliefs, if (and only if) it recognizes and exercises its sovereignty. Without that recognition, that mind is conditioned and enslaved by the Storyline (Velcro-ed™). It's as simple as that. But simple is not the same thing as easy!

You exist apart from the Storyline of your life – this is the heart of all spiritual Truth. The Storyline is tremendously engaging, and when we become "Velcro-ed™" to it, we forget our independent existence and come to identify with the Storyline. But you are so much more than just the sum of your Storyline and biological parts!

Your True Essence, your Inner Unlimited Self, transcends all boundaries of biology and narrative. Your Inner Self is not conditioned by others or circumstances.

When you identify with the Inner Self rather than the Ego Self, you allow yourself greater access to higher vibratory states unavailable to the Limited Self of the Ego. The trick is to remember this on a day-to-day, moment-by-moment basis.

Everything in the Storyline conspires to keep you "Velcro-ed™" to it. At this stage in your Inner Self's evolution, the Limited Self cannot but help to get "Velcro-ed™." Expect it, accept it, but then be willing to move beyond the Storyline, no matter how compelling or frightening.

By remembering you have a choice of which aspect of yourself you identify with, you make those options live for you. You get to choose the quality of your Storyline, if not the content. You get to choose what kind of character and setting you will play.

But never forget that you are much more than just a character in a specific setting with certain personality traits and challenges – you are an aspect of the Universe – a part of a much vaster whole. When you remember this, you are able to identify with All That Is, and to not be restricted to the confines of the Limited Self and its Storylines.

Only this is the Real Choice, the True Freedom. All other choices and liberties within the Storyline are trivial and meaningless from the perspective of the Inner Self. Yet we become entranced and attached to the seeming myriad of choices and decisions of the Storyline – apportioning blame, guilt, fear, desire and regret to them and working ourselves into a tizzy.

And we call this Free Will, but it is anything but free! This is not Freedom nor Will. This is the illusion of Choice and Free Will.

Choosing between brands of toothpaste or toilet paper at the grocery store is not a true Choice of being. Choosing particular individual expressions of biological mandates are not Free Will. Knee-jerk reactions to crises are not Free Will.

Only the Choice of Identification is unconstrained. You may not have complete liberty in your choice of work, location or family. Even your choice of mate is constrained by proximity and access (not to mention compatibility). Your biology is determined by inherited genetics and the environment in which you were brought up, neither of which you had a say in.

The only thing you do have total control over is who you choose to be in this present moment. You don't have the ability to change the past (unless you've been doing some serious inner work) and only limited ability to change the future (until you do some serious inner work). And you definitely can't change your future as long as you are "Velcro-ed™" to the dramas of your Storyline.

Only the choice to focus on and identify with the Inner Self releases the "Velcro™." Only by embracing the Inner Self can we find True Free Will. Only at the level of the Inner Self are we able to escape the determinism of the Storyline and to know Real Liberty and Self-Determination.

Real Liberty is not granted by any government. Real Liberty cannot be taken away. Real Liberty demands no sacrifices of blood and resources. Real Liberty cannot be threatened in any external way, because Real Liberty lies within your own consciousness.

The only person or thing that can deny you your 'Being Right' of Liberty is you – either through ignorance or through fear. No one else can make you who you are, and attempts to blame others for the quality of our existence are disingenuous at best, and irresponsible cowardice at worst. Only you can choose who you want to be at any given moment.

But it is up to you to remember this and to choose the Inner Self over the Storyline... again and again and yet again. No one else can do this for you, for if they did, you would not have Free Will. The only way to transcend the Limited Self and its Storyline is to make it a priority in your life to remember the One Choice of Identity.

At any given moment, you can choose to come from the False Self of Ego or to come from your Inner Self. But you must remember that you have a choice for it to be a live option for you. Therefore, surround yourself with reminders of your Inner Self – art, jewelry, books, whatever works to jog your memory that you are an Unlimited Creature in Ultimate Reality. It is worth the effort!

The Inner Self is YOU, without effort, without fear and without regret. Your Inner Self does not have to try to live up to the standards and expectations of others. Your Inner Self has made no errors in the past and cannot go wrong in the future. It is beyond the Storyline's criteria for right and wrong.

Fear, regret and time are all artifacts of the Storyline. The Inner Self transcends and is beyond all aspects and claims of the Storyline. The Inner Self is pure existential bliss, without comparisons, competition or efforting of any kind. It is pure being in your own unique idiom, that seeks nothing because it is already complete, and no one's approval could add one iota to it's completeness. Indeed, the Inner Self does not need to seek at all, for it already contains the fullness of All That You Are. Nothing more can be added and nothing can be removed.

In contrast, the Limited Self seeks the approval of others to survive. The Limited Self competes and frets over the possibility of failure and endings. But the Inner Self cannot end, for it cannot be limited, by definition. Eternally changeless, your Inner Self's perfection has always existed and always will be. There is nothing your Limited Self can do to change or alter the perfection of the Inner Self. Your Inner Self is beyond both words and thought.

Your Inner Self does not make or do anything – it simply IS. It's perfection is not founded in action or intention – its perfection is a manifestation of Universal Grace, and so is therefore beyond the reach of the Limited Self to corrupt or pollute or destroy.

When we choose to identify with the Inner Self rather than the Limited Self, we allow ourselves access to higher vibratory rates, and in this manner , we throw off the "Velcro™" of the Storyline. Therefore, it is imperative to access the Inner Self as often as possible if you would escape the confines of your personal Storyline.

It is my hope that the ideas and suggestions in this book are of use to you. Exploring the Inner Self is the greatest adventure you can ever have!

BIBLIOGRAPHY

(Author's Note: Some of these were referred to in the essays, other books are simply ones I believe anyone serious about Subjective Reality should look into. Enjoy!)

Alder, Vera Stanley, *Finding of the Third Eye.* Samuel Weiser, Inc. York Beach, ME 1938/1970

Aristotle, *The Nicomachean Ethics.* Hackett Publishing Co, Indianapolis, IN 1985 Trans. Terence Irwin

Bach, Richard, *Illusions: The Adventures of a Reluctant Messiah.* Dell Publishing/Random House 1977

Bailey, Alice A., *Initiation, Human and Solar.* Lucis Publishing Co. NY 1922/1977

Bennett, John G., *Making A Soul: Human Destiny and the Debt of Our Existence.* Bennett Books, Santa Fe, NM 1995

Bennett, John G., *The Masters of Wisdom – An Esoteric History of the Spiritual Unfolding of Life on This Planet.* Bennett Books, Santa Fe, NM 1995

Berkeley, George, *Principles of Human Knowledge/ Three Dialogues.* London, New York, Australia, Toronto, New Zealand. Penguin Books 1988

Bloom, Allan, ed. *The Republic of Plato.* 1968 Basic Books, New York

Brodie, Richard, *Virus of the Mind – The New Science of the Meme.* Integral Press, Seattle 1996

Buber, Martin, *I and Thou.* New York City, New York, MacMillan Publishing Co. 1987

Bucke, Richard M., MD. *Cosmic Consciousness - a Study in the Evolution of the Human Mind.* New Hyde Park, NY. University Books, Inc. 1961

Dennett, Daniel, *Consciousness Explained.* London, New York, Australia, Toronto, New Zealand. Penguin Books 1991

DeRopp, Robert S., *The Master Game, Pathways to Higher Consciousness Beyond the Drug Experience.* Delta/Seymour Lawrence Books, New York 1968

Fortune, Dion, *The Cosmic Doctrine.* Samuel Weiser, York Beach, Maine 1976

Fortune, Dion, *The Mystical Qabbalah.* Samuel Weiser, York, Beach, Maine. 1935

Fortune, Dion, *The Training and Work of an Initiate.* Samuel Weiser York, Beach, Maine 1967/2000

Foundation for Inner Peace, *A Course in Miracles.* Foundation for Inner Peace 1975

Frankl, Viktor F., *Man's Search for Meaning.* Washington Square Press/Simon & Schuster, Boston, MA 1946

Gall, John, *Systemantics: How Systems Work and Especially How They Fail.* Quadrangle/New York Times Books YN 1975

Grof, Stanislav, *The Holotropic Mind.* New York. Harper Publishing Co. 1993

Gurdjieff, G. I., *Beelzebub's Tales to His Grandson: An Objectively Impartial Criticism of the Life of Man.* Routledge & Kegan Paul, London 1950

Gurdjieff, G.I., *Views From the Real World*. New York. E.P. Dutton 1975

Hesse, Hermann, *Siddhartha – An Indian Tale*. Penguin Books, NY 1999 Trans. Joachim Neugroschel

Jaynes, Julian, *The Origin of Consciousness in the Breakdown of the Bicameral Mind.* Houghton Mifflin Books, Boston MA 1976/1990

Johnson, Robert A., *Inner Work – Using Dreams and Active Imagination for Personal Growth.* 1986, Harper and Row, San Francisco, Cambridge, Hagerstown, New York, Philadelphia, London, Mexico City, Sao Paulo, Singapore, Sydney

Johnson, Robert A., *Owning Your Own Shadow.* HarperCollins Publishers, San Francisco 1991

Jung, C.G., *Memories, Dreams, Reflections.* 1961 Vintage Books, New York

Jung, C.G., *The Undiscovered Self,* 1957 Mentor Books, Boston, MA

Khan, Hazrat Inayat, *Sufi Teachings: The Art of Being.* Element Books, Shaftsbury, Dorsett, UK and Rockport, Maine, USA

Khan, Hazrat Inayat, *The Inner Life.* Shambhala Books, Boston & London 1997

Leary, Timothy, *The Game of Life,* 1979 New Falcon Publications, Phoenix, AZ

Leary, Timothy, *Info-Psychology – A Manual on the Use of the Human Nervous System According to the Instructions of the*

Manufacturers. 1987 Falcon Press, Los Vegas

Lilly, John C., *The Center of the Cyclone - an Autobiography of Inner Space* New York, Toronto, London. Bantam Books 1972.

Lilly, John C., *The Deep Self – Profound Relaxation and the Tank Isolation Technique,* 1977. Warner Books, New York

Lilly, John C., *Programming and Metaprogramming in the Human Biocomputer.* 1967. Julian Press, New York

McKenna, Jed, *Spiritual Enlightenment: The Damnedest Thing.* 2002 Wisefool Press USA

McKenna, Terence, *Food of the Gods: The Search for the Original Tree of Knowledge.* Bantam Books, NY 1992

Merrill-Wolff, Franklin, *The Philosophy of Consciousness Without an Object - Reflections on the Nature of Transcendental Consciousness.* New York. Julian Press 1973

Ouspensky, P.D., *The Psychology of Man's Possible Evolution.* Vintage Books/Random House, NY 1950

Pascal, Blaise. *Pensees and Other Writings.* Trans. by Honor Levi Oxford, New York. Oxford University Press. 1995

Pearce, Joseph Chilton, *The Biology of Transcendence: A Blueprint of the Human Spirit.* Park Street Press, Rochester, Vermont 2002

Pearce, Joseph Chilton. *Evolution's End - Claiming the Potential of Our Intelligence.* San Francisco Harper 1993

Pearce, Joseph Chilton. *The Crack in the Cosmic Egg: Challenging Constructs of Mind and Reality.* Washington Square Books, NY 1971

Pinker, Steven. *The Blank Slate – the Modern Denial of Human Nature*, 2002 Viking Press, New York, London, England, Victoria, Australia, Toronto, Canada, New Delhi, India, Auckland, New Zealand, Johannesburg, South Africa

Quinn, Daniel, *Ishmael: An Adventure of the Mind and Spirit.* Bantam Books/Random House 1992

Roberts, Jane and Seth, *The Nature of Personal Reality.* Bantam Books, Toronto, NY, London 1974

Rosenberg, Alexander. *Philosophy of Social Science.* 1988 Westview Press, Boulder, CO, Oxford, England

Sanford, John A., *The Invisible Partners – How the Male and Female in Each of Us Affects Our Relationships.* 1980 Paulist Press, New York

Scheinfeld, Robert, *The 11th Element: The Key to Unlocking Your Master Blueprint for Wealth and Success.* John Wiley & Sons, Inc. Hoboken, NJ 2003

Taylor, Charles. *The Ethics of Authenticity.* 1991 Harvard University Press, Cambridge, MA, London, England

Taylor, Charles. *Sources of the Self – The Making of Modern Identity.* 1989 Harvard University Press, Cambridge, MA

Thompson, William Irwin, *The Time Falling Bodies Take to Light – Mythology, Sexuality and the Origins of Culture.* St. Martin's Press, NY 1981

Tolle, Eckhart, *The Power of Now.* New World Library, Novato, CA & Vancouver, Canada 1999/2004

Watts, Alan, *Become What You Are.* Shambhala Books, Boston & London 1995/2003

Wilson, Robert Anton, *Cosmic Trigger: The Final Secret of the Illuminati.* Pocket Books/Simon & Schuster, NY 1977

Wilson, Robert Anton. *Prometheus Rising.* New Falcon Press, Tempe, AZ 1983

Wilson, Robert Anton. *Quantum Psychology: How Brain Software Programs You and Your World.* New Falcon Press, Phoenix, AZ 1990

Yogananda, Paramahamsa. *Autobiography of a Yogi.* 1973 Self-Realization Fellowship, Los Angeles, CA

Zukav, Gary, *The Seat of the Soul.* New York, London, Toronto, Sydney, Tokyo, Singapore. Simon & Schuster 1990

SOME HELPFUL LINKS

Dara Fogel's Website: http://www.provinceofthemind.com

On Objective Reality: http://www.iep.utm.edu/objectiv/

On Subjective Reality:
http://www.stevepavlina.com/blog/2007/09/subjectiv
e-reality-simplified/

On Monism: http://en.wikipedia.org/wiki/Monism

On Solipsism: http://www.iep.utm.edu/solipsis/

On How the Human Consciousness Works:
http://www.psychologytoday.com/blog/the-
superhuman-mind/201303/what-is-consciousness

On A Scientist's Perspective on Consciousness:
http://thebrainbank.scienceblog.com/2013/03/04/wh
at-is-consciousness-a-scientists-perspective/

On Intersubjective Agreement:
http://en.wikipedia.org/wiki/Intersubjectivity

On Gnosis: http://en.wikipedia.org/wiki/Gnosis

On Cartesian Dualism:
http://www.allaboutphilosophy.org/cartesian-
dualism-faq.htm

On Near-Death-Experiences (NDE):
http://www.nderf.org/index.htm

On Out-of-Body-Experiences (OBE):
http://science.howstuffworks.com/science-vs-myth/extrasensory-
perceptions/out-of-body-experience.htm

The Impossible Lover by Dara Fogel:
http://www.amazon.com/The-Impossible-Lover-GrailChase-Chronicles-ebook/dp/B00H08TENO/ref=zg_bs_6361472011_f_5

On the Unconscious:
http://www.psychologytoday.com/basics/unconscious

On Determinism:
http://www.informationphilosopher.com/freedom/determinism.html

On G.I. Gurdjieff: http://www.gurdjieff.org/sayings.htm

On Plato and the Tripartite Soul:
http://plato.stanford.edu/entries/ancient-soul/

On Sigmund Freud: http://www.iep.utm.edu/freud/

On Carl Jung: http://en.wikipedia.org/wiki/Carl_Jung

On Social Constructivism:
http://plato.stanford.edu/entries/social-construction-naturalistic/

On Steven Pinker: http://stevenpinker.com/

On Charles Taylor:
http://www.mcgill.ca/philosophy/people/faculty/taylor

On Timothy Leary: http://www.timothyleary.us/

On John Lilly: http://www.johnclilly.com/

On Richard M. Bucke's Cosmic Consciousness:
https://archive.org/details/cosmconscious

On The Fourth Way:
http://en.wikipedia.org/wiki/Fourth_Way

On Olaf Stapledon's The Star Maker:
http://en.wikipedia.org/wiki/Star_Maker

On Advaita Hinduism:
http://en.wikipedia.org/wiki/Advaita_Vedanta

On Universals: http://plato.stanford.edu/entries/nominalism-metaphysics/

On Particulars: http://en.wikipedia.org/wiki/Particular

On George Berkeley: http://www.iep.utm.edu/berkeley/

On Stanislav Grof: http://www.stanislavgrof.com/

On Qabbalah: http://en.wikipedia.org/wiki/Hermetic_Qabalah

On Virtue Ethics:
http://stanford.library.usyd.edu.au/entries/ethics-virtue/

On Eudaemonia:
http://www.britannica.com/EBchecked/topic/194966/eudaimonia

ABOUT THE AUTHOR

Dara Fogel is an author, philosopher and educator. She lives in the American Southwest with her husband, mother, son, two cats, a dog and a fish. She holds a Ph.D. in Philosophy from the University of Oklahoma, specializing in Ethics, Social-Political Philosophy and Philosophy of the Self.

After surviving a life-threatening bout of encephalitis and spinal meningitis her sophomore year in college, she sustained brain damage and lost the ability to walk and talk, along with large chunks of her memory. Although her neurologist gave her a dire prognosis, something within refused to accept the opinions and statistics of the experts.

Instead, she sought out alternative treatments, including Chinese Medicine, Juicing and Cranial-Sacral Therapy, and made what her doctors called "a remarkable recovery." She used her college Performance Arts and Dance classes to help her learn to re-connect to and use her body.

During this time, she began having spontaneous out-of-body experiences, including encounters with her own Deep Being. She ended up changing her major and getting her doctorate in Philosophy (which included a four year stint as a graduate assistant in a Religious Studies Program) as a result of pursuing the burning questions left behind by her experiences.

Much of her writing, including the six-part GrailChase Chronicles series, was written as a means to grapple with, explore and develop her own Subjective Reality.

OTHER WORKS BY DARA FOGEL

Before the Chase: A Short Anthology

Three sassy and sexy prequel tales from the GrailChase Chronicles series. #1 Bestselling Free Steampunk and #1 Bestselling Free Science Fiction Anthology on Amazon Kindle. Available Now at Amazon & Smashwords

The Impossible Lover
Book One of the GrailChase Chronicles

"The DaVinci Code meets Steampunk, with Dune flavor crystals."
A Subjective Reality Steampunk Conspiracy Theory Romance. A story of awakening consciousness, soulmates and strange gadgets.
#1 Bestselling Free Steampunk and #3 Bestselling Metaphysical and Visionary Science Fiction on Amazon Kindle. Available Now at Amazon & Smashwords

Coming Soon:
Herald of the Dawn
Book Two of the GrailChase Chronicles

In the aftermath of their forbidden affair, Haldane and Sophia have to deal with the unintended consequences of their choices. Cameos from Oscar Wilde and Madame Helena Blavatsky help guide the way.
Due Spring 2014

CONNECT WITH DARA ONLINE

Website: www.province-of-the-mind.com
Blog: http://www.province-of-the-mind.com/personal-development.xml
Twitter: @aferalgod
Also on Facebook

www.ingramcontent.com/pod-product-compliance
Lightning Source LLC
LaVergne TN
LVHW021358080426
835508LV00020B/2342